From
DEVASTATION
To
RESTORATION

JERRY SAVELLE

FROM DEVASTATION TO RESTORATION

ISBN 0-9655352-2-3
Unless otherwise stated, all scripture
quotations are taken from
The King James Version of the Bible.

Jerry Savelle Publications
P.O. Box 748
Crowley, TX 76036
817/297-3155

✿ ✿ TABLE OF CONTENTS ✿ ✿

CHAPTER 1   Time's Up, Devil -- God's Taking Over! - Page 9

CHAPTER 2   Are You Fed Up, Yet? - Page 21

CHAPTER 3   God Wants to do Something New in
Your Life - Page 37

CHAPTER 4   Changing Your Atmosphere - Page 49

CHAPTER 5   If You Can Conceive It, You Can
Receive It - Page 63

CHAPTER 6   Staying Positive in a Negative World - Page 75

CHAPTER 7   Delays: Why They Happen & How to Deal
With Them - Page 87

CHAPTER 8   In Every Great Storm There Is a Great
Victory - Page 103

CHAPTER 9   Develop a Restoration Mentality - Page 119

CHAPTER 10   God's Way of Restoration - Page 133

CHAPTER 11   Changing Your Outlook - Page 147

CHAPTER 12   The Best is Yet To Come - Page 159

CHAPTER 1

CHAPTER 1

Time's Up, Devil - God's Taking Over!

When I was growing up in school, I was always the smallest boy in the class. Most of the girls were bigger than me! From the first grade all the way through high school I was known as "Little Jerry".

I hated it. If you were little like me, then you got picked on and pushed around. You got bullied by all the big guys.

My Dad always told me, "Son, if I ever catch you starting a fight, I'm going to whip you. If I ever catch you running from a fight, I'm going to whip you."

Well, I knew I wouldn't get a whipping for starting any because I wasn't big enough to start fights. So I got pushed and bullied around almost every day, but there finally came a time when I got fed up with it.

Finally, I told that bully, "Time's up!!" He didn't think I meant it. I said, "That's it! You're not going to push me around anymore. I'm tired of you embarrassing me in front of the class. Time's up!"

He laughed and turned to all the kids standing around watching and said, "Did you hear what Little Jerry said?"

Before he got completely turned around again, there was a fist in his nose! I caught him off guard. Much to his surprise (and mine), he landed on his back. I didn't know I had this kind of power in me. I saw him on the ground with his nose bleeding so I just jumped right in the middle of his chest and finished the job. He was begging me to leave him alone, but I said, "Too bad - time's up! I'm taking over now!" And you know what? He never bothered me again.

I believe it's time for us to tell the devil, "Time's up! You have plagued me long enough! You've kept me bound up long enough! You've kept me strapped with debt long enough! You've tried to destroy my home, my marriage, and my family, but your time is up in this house, devil - God is taking over!"

I don't know what you may be going through right now, but it's time for you to get fed up. Get fed up with Satan stealing from you. Get fed up with him robbing your joy, destroying your family, and shattering your dreams.

Nothing will change in your life until you absolutely get fed up with your present condition. Satan will continue to destroy your life until you get in his face and say, "Time's up, devil — God's taking over!"

Satan is out to devastate your life. What is *devastation?* It is defined as: to destroy or ruin; to overwhelm or overpower.

Whatever you're going through right now is not too big for God to handle. This may be hard for you to understand, but you are not the only person who has ever gone through what you're going through. And obviously, God thinks you're capable of going through it and coming out victorious. Now you've got to see yourself that way!

THERE'S A WHOLE LOTTA SHAKIN' GOING ON!

Get ready because when God takes over, He's going to shake up some things that men think can't be shaken. He's going to pull down some things that men think can't be pulled down. I like to say it this way - Satan's days are numbered!

Notice what God says will happen when the Anointed One comes on the scene.

> *And it shall come to pass in that day, that his burden shall be taken away from off thy shoulder, and his yoke from off thy neck, and the yoke shall be destroyed because of the anointing.*

> Isaiah 10:27

You ought to write in the margin of your Bible, "He will bust Satan's head!" I know the correct word is "burst" but it doesn't work here. "Bust" sounds better. The anointing will destroy, not break, but destroy every yoke from off your neck and leave no evidence that there was ever a yoke there!

What is God saying to the adversary? "Time's up!" Once again, we read what the Anointing will do when it comes on the scene.

> *The Spirit of the Lord God is upon me because the Lord has anointed me to preach good tidings unto the meek; he hath sent me to bind up the broken-hearted, to proclaim liberty to the captives, and the opening of the prison to them that are bound;*

FROM DEVASTATION TO RESTORATION

To proclaim the acceptable year of the Lord, and the day of vengeance of our God; to comfort all that mourn;

To appoint unto them that mourn in Zion, to give unto them beauty for ashes, the oil of joy for mourning, the garment of praise for the spirit of heaviness; that they might be called trees of righteousness.

Isaiah 61:1-3

God is saying, "I'm going to turn your mourning into dancing, turn your sorrow into joy, and take that old garment of heaviness off of you and put on the garment of praise!"

What is God announcing? "Satan, your time's up, I'm taking over!! You have had them bound up long enough."

In Psalm 126, notice what happens when God decrees that Satan's time is up and He turns the captivity of His people.

When the Lord turned again the captivity of Zion, we were like them that dream.

Then was our mouth filled with laughter, and our tongue with singing...

They that sow in tears shall reap in joy.

Psalm 126:1-2, 5

Our mouths will be filled with laughter and singing? Well, I don't know if you've noticed lately, but there are a lot of manifestations of laughter and singing in the Body of Christ! Sounds like to me that's an indication that the devil's time is up!!

I was reading my Message Translation of the Bible and I got a big kick out of Matthew 8:28-29. It says,

"They landed in the country of the Gadarenes and were met by two madmen, victims of demons, coming out of the cemetery. The men had terrorized the region for so long that no one considered it safe to walk down that stretch of road anymore. Seeing Jesus, the madmen screamed out, 'What business do you have giving us a hard time? You're the Son of God! You weren't supposed to show up here yet!'"

The shakeup has begun, and the demons are going

to be crying out from here on out because their time is up! They're going to be crying out, "You weren't supposed to show up yet, Jesus! I haven't destroyed them yet!" Jesus caught them off guard here and He's going to catch them off guard in your behalf!!

The Bible says, *The wealth of the sinner is laid up for the just.* The Amplified says, *...eventually into the hands of the righteous, for whom it was laid up* (Proverbs 13:22). I hear God saying, "Time's up, devil, I'm taking charge of the finances! Eventually has come!!" So start walking around with expectancy because it's going to come into your hands!!

You may be saying, "But Brother Jerry, I'm under the greatest pressure I've ever experienced."

That's an indication that you've got the devil right where you want him. His time's up!!

If you're thinking, "I can't stand anymore - you don't realize what's happened in my life," - Rejoice!! Satan's time is up!

This is not the time to quit! No! You've come too far to quit, glory to God; you are about to win.

God is going to give your adversary a hard time

from here on out, Hallelujah! Whatever is troubling you and trying to destroy you - don't worry about it! God's working behind the scenes. Demons are trembling right now! Oh, they are shaking! There are alarms going off in Satan's domain! They hear God's voice crying out, "Time's up!"

IT'S TIME TO SEND 'EM PACKING!

The greatest harvest, the greatest miracles, the greatest manifestations, and the greatest financial blessings are upon us! Time's up where the devil is concerned! It's your time now!

> *"Everyone there was incredulous, buzzing with curiosity. 'What's going on here? A new teaching that does what it says? He shuts up defiling, demonic spirits and sends them packing!'"*
>
> Mark 1:27 (The Message)

That old demon of lack in your life is going to pack up and move out! That old demon of sickness and disease is going to pack up and leave, Hallelujah! You know why? Because time's up around your house! God's issuing a war cry again. The signs of the times are indicating to us that the Anointed One is about to make another appearance.

...Resist the devil and he will flee from you.

James 4:7

The Message translation says it this way,

"So let God work his will in you. Yell a loud NO to the Devil and watch him scamper. Say a quiet YES to God and he'll be there in no time."

What's God saying? It's time to quit playing church. It's time to quit playing religious games. Humble yourself before the mighty hand of God, resist the devil and he will flee from you. Get fed up where the devil is concerned!

Satan's not going to have his way in your life any more. He's going to be packing up and moving out! I challenge you to shout at the devil right now and just let him know how fed up you are with him trying to destroy your life. Let him know that as of today, he will no longer have his way in your household - his time is up! Make a declaration of faith and stick to it - his days are numbered. The Anointed One is about to make another appearance, so get ready! As far as you're concerned, God's turning this devastation in your life into restoration! Hallelujah!

CHAPTER 2

CHAPTER 2

Are You Fed Up, Yet?

As I've already mentioned, before anything will change in your life, you've got to get fed up with your present condition. God is wanting to raise up an army of believers in these last days who will literally march into Satan's camp and take back everything he has stolen! But you've got to get fed up with the devil stealing everything you've got! You've got to get fed up with never having enough and fed up with always coming up short! It's time for supernatural increase and restoration in your life.

These are exciting times! Supernatural increase and restoration are in the air, and God wants you to be affected by it. He wants it happening to you! It's happening to all those who will get in position to receive.

This is a new day, and Satan is running scared. He knows there is an army rising up in the earth today that is militant. We have become aggressive! We have made up our minds that we are going to get back everything that's been stolen from us. You may as well become a part of it.

Deception:
Satan's Mightiest Weapon

When you are entitled to be blessed, the only way Satan can keep you from experiencing that blessing is through deception. Deception is Satan's mightiest weapon. Outside of deception, Satan is helpless. If he can't deceive you, he can't defeat you. If he can't deceive you, he can't steal from you. According to the Word, one of the ways he deceives the Body of Christ is through a lack of knowledge.

My people are destroyed for lack of knowledge.

Hosea 4:6

If you don't know that you have a right to live in health, you will live in sickness. If you don't know you have a right to prosper, you will live in poverty and defeat. If you don't know you have a right to be delivered, you will live in bondage. But the moment you find out the truth, the truth will set you free. You will begin to walk in the blessing that you are entitled to.

FROM DEVASTATION TO RESTORATION

Obviously, Satan doesn't want you to find out what rightfully belongs to you as a child of God, and he will do everything in his power to keep you in darkness. How? Through deception.

God's done everything that is necessary for you and I to live an overcoming life. Jesus does not have to go to the cross again for that to take place in your life. He's already gone. He's already made provision. He's already given His Word. He's already shed His blood. The covenant is in effect, and all you have to do is get in position to receive, stand your ground, and don't let the devil steal your blessing.

Let me ask you a question. Have you ever had a blessing stolen from you? There are a number of ways that Satan will attack you hoping that you'll drop your guard so he can steal your blessing.

I grew up in the country, as we say, I'm a farm boy. And I wanted my kids to grow up in that kind of environment. They weren't that thrilled about it, but I wanted them to be around horses and cattle and the soil.

We didn't have a ranch, we had a "ranchette." I had a bull named Elijah that acted like a dog. He followed me everywhere I went. Later, I got another bull named Samson and a heifer named Mary. Soon we had a little Joshua. My herd grew to about fifteen.

Then, we got into horses. I bought a horse for every member of the family. Well, then you've got to have saddles. You've got to have a barn and stables. I mean, we really got into this thing. Finally, my accountant said, "This is no longer a hobby, Jerry. You are now the owner of the 4 S Ranch." I was loving it!

Then a man made me a beautiful saddle for my horse, Jubilee. And one day, somebody broke into my tack room and stole all my saddles. It's a good thing I wasn't around. I don't know what I'd have done to that guy if I would have caught him.

I can't stand a thief and that bothered me for weeks. I've been known to give things away, but when he came on my property, broke into my tack room, and stole my saddles...the fire of God was in my eyes and I don't know what was in my flesh, but it was fiery, too. I just can't stand a thief. Mainly because he has no regard for what I went through to acquire what he just stole from me.

The Lord said to me, "I've never seen you so mad." I said, "I'm real mad. If I could catch him..." He said, "Why don't you act that way about the devil?" I said,

"We're not talking about the devil right now. I want that guy." He said, "The devil steals from you, and you let him get away with it. I'm surprised at the way you're reacting to this."

He said, "You're so mad you can hardly see straight. You're hoping he'll come back, just so you can get revenge." He said, "I've never ever seen you this way where the devil is concerned and he's stealing from you every day." I suddenly realized what God was saying to me.

The devil is stealing from the Body of Christ! Some members just give up and let him do it. They don't even put up a fight. The devil's stealing off of us, and we just sit there and let him get away with it.

God says,

But if he be found, he shall restore sevenfold.

Proverbs 6:31

If you'll begin making the devil pay it all back, it will finally get to the point, that you will get too expensive for the devil to mess with! Satan's got warehouses full of what belongs to the Body of Christ. He's got buildings that belong to us. He's got transportation vehicles that belong to us. He's got equipment that belongs to us. He's got finances that belong to us.

Remember the story of two brothers, Jacob and Esau? Jacob stole his brother's birthright and his blessing, and notice what Isaac says to Esau concerning his future:

> *And by thy sword shalt thou live, and shalt serve thy brother; and it shall come to pass when thou shalt have the dominion, that thou shalt break his yoke from off thy neck.*

Genesis 27:40

There is a deceiver in the earth, and if you are ever going to get back what he's stolen from you, you're going to have to live by the sword. That sword is not a defensive weapon, it is an offensive weapon! If you are passive, you'll never get your blessing back. You've got to be militant. You've got to be assertive. You've got to be aggressive, or you'll never get your blessing back.

...And it shall come to pass... Don't you love that? If you will live by your sword, which is the Word of God, then you can count on it; this will come to pass:

...when thou shalt have the dominion, that thou shalt break his yoke from off thy neck. Now what's God saying here? He says if you'll determine that you are going to live by your sword, you're going to live by the Word of God, then there will come a time that you will move over into a position of dominion, and you'll break that yoke from off your neck which literally means: Satan has to repay what he has stolen from you, hallelujah!! The New American Standard says it this way:

> *And by your sword you shall live, And your brother you shall serve...*

God says, "I'm going to reverse some things. Instead of you being under subordination to the deceiver, I'll reverse it, and the deceiver will now be under your dominion. Instead of the devil controlling your life, you're controlling his. Instead of him making you miserable every day, you're making him miserable every day."

> *...And your brother you shall serve, but it shall come about when you become restless...*

The Savelle translation for "you shall become restless," is "fed up!" Do you ever get fed up over something every once in a while? What happens when you reach the point of being "fed up?" There is an anointing that comes on you. There is a dominion that you begin to walk in and everybody within shouting distance knows you are fed up.

What happens when you're fed up? You move into action. Then what happens? You start getting results. Have you ever noticed what happens when a mother tells her children to clean up their room repeatedly and they don't respond?

She tells those precious little angels, "I want you to clean up that room!!" She comes back later and nothing has changed. "I said, clean up the room!" she says.

Eventually, she returns to find that still nothing has changed! What happens? Mama gets fed up! And when mama gets fed up, there is an anointing that comes on her. Her countenance changes. Her voice changes. Her dominion takes over. She is changed into another woman. All of a sudden she is no longer the weaker vessel. It is Samson in disguise. The kids know when mama is fed up. I don't care if her husband weighs 272 pounds and whips everybody in the neighborhood, when mama is fed up, he becomes a lamb. What happened? She has reached the point of no return, and then she gets results.

You may not be fed up yet with Satan stealing from you. You could be politely saying, "Oh God, make the devil get off me!" He won't. The devil won't get off of you until you get fed up with him being on you!

You're not going to change your lifestyle until you are fed up with the way you are living. You have to be fed up with your kids being on drugs. You have to be fed up with your mate going to hell. But the moment you get fed up, things will change!

When you get fed up, you're going to take that yoke off your neck! When you get fed up, there isn't any demon in hell that can hold you back! As long as you are still tolerating it, you're not fed up! Don't just accept your condition. Don't make provision for failure. Instead of petting the problem, get fed up with it!

When I say fed up, I'm not talking about "psyching" yourself out. No! I'm not talking about sitting in your bedroom and getting psyched up and saying, "I'm fed up. I'm fed up...." That isn't going to do you any good. The only way you are going to get truly spiritually fed up is through the entrance of His Word! Because with the entrance of His Word, you begin to realize who you are in Christ and your authority over the devil.

When you find out what is yours by revelation of the Word of God, you will never be passive again. Why? Because you are fed up! You'll be declaring, "No more, Satan! This is where you get out! You aren't welcome here anymore! You can take your sickness and your disease and go in the Name of Jesus! Take your hands off my family! Take your hands off my body! Take your hands off my finances! Take your hands off everything that is mine! You are history, devil, and you're not welcome here anymore!"

And then get back what's been stolen! Don't let the devil off the hook. Make him pay it all back sevenfold!

Pursue, Overtake and Recover All!

Let me show you what God is expecting you to do from a story in the Bible. When we find out that it's Satan stealing our blessings, then it's time for us to get into action.

In I Samuel 30, we read of David and his men who returned to find that their homes had been burned to the ground, and the enemy had taken their wives and children.

Can you imagine how this man must have felt?

FROM DEVASTATION TO RESTORATION

The dearest thing to him has been stolen. His privacy has been invaded. Read what the Word says about David.

> *Then David and the people that were with him lifted up their voice and wept, until they had no more power to weep.*
>
> *And David's two wives were taken captives, Ahinoam the Jezreelitess, and Abigail the wife of Nabal the Carmelite.*
>
> *And David was greatly distressed; for the people spake of stoning him because the soul of all the people was grieved, every man for his sons and for his daughters: but David encouraged himself in the Lord his God.*
>
> I Samuel 30:4-6

After they got through crying, they all started blaming David. They wanted to stone him. I would imagine that David is sitting there thinking, "Well, I deserve to be stoned. Put me out of my misery. I did not ask for this. I was happy when I was herding sheep. If God would have left me alone out there in that pasture, this wouldn't have happened."

Right in the middle of all this, something changed. The Word says, **David encouraged himself in the Lord.** Right in the midst of all the distress, David said, "Wait a minute! I don't have to tolerate this! I don't have to put up with this."

He could have sat there, given up and quit, but he made up his mind, "No, it's not over just because the enemy has come in and stolen my property. It's not over! It's never over until God says its over, hallelujah! God delivered me before, and He'll deliver me now."

You've got to reach a point where you grow restless, and make up your mind that you are not staying this way anymore and begin encouraging yourself in the Lord. Don't wait around for someone else to encourage you. There may not be anybody else. YOU have to encourage yourself! David went from distressed to wanting to fight.

> *And David inquired at the Lord, saying, Shall I pursue after this troop? shall I overtake them? And he answered him, Pursue: for thou shalt surely overtake them, and without fail recover all.*
>
> I Samuel 30:8

FROM DEVASTATION TO RESTORATION

When the enemy has stolen from you, not only does God want you to get up and pursue the enemy, but He wants you to literally march into His camp and recover all! God's not satisfied with you only getting up and being aggressive. He wants you to get back what was stolen.

That's exactly what David did. He pursued the enemy, he overtook him, and he recovered all! I believe our marching orders from our commander are: "Pursue, overtake, and recover all!" God's wanting an army of people to rise up and get back what's been stolen from them. Are you fed up, yet? Start taking action today!

CHAPTER 3

CHAPTER 3

God Wants to do Something New in Your Life

In 1981, as I was preaching for Brother Kenneth Copeland in Charlotte, North Carolina in the Believers' Convention, I received a supernatural visitation of the Lord.

In that visitation, the Lord began to minister to me concerning how the body of Christ could get out of financial famine. For several years, everywhere I went God had me preaching on how to overcome financial famine.

Then some major scandals broke out in ministries, and here I was preaching all over the world about prosperity and financial deliverance.

So I told the Lord, "Now Father, I've been very diligent about protecting this ministry, and building it on integrity. We're established, we're respected, and I don't want the media to get the idea that we're involved in the same kind of misconduct that was brought about in these scandals." So I said, "If it's all right with You, I'm just going to put this financial teaching You've given me on the shelf, and I'll preach some other things until all of this blows over." And He never said, "That's fine, son." He never said, "I rebuke thee." He didn't say anything. I came up with a plan. He just sat there and listened. And for the next five years, it was the most miserable five years I've ever spent. Somebody said, "Oh the price to be in the will of God." I can tell you how much it cost to be out. It was tough. We survived, but that wasn't God's best.

Then in November of 1992 while I was preaching with Brother Copeland in the International Believers' Convention in Bournemouth, England, I received another visitation of the Lord. And in this visitation, He instructed me to challenge the body of Christ everywhere I go to get out of a survival mentality and begin to believe Him for supernatural increase and restoration.

I have been preaching this everywhere because I have a mandate. The Lord instructed me to do it. This time He said, "If you don't preach what I'm telling you, I won't ask you again, I'll call on somebody else." I said, "You don't have to be concerned about that, my plans don't work. I'm going to go with Yours."

So I have been faithful to preach it all over the world in every continent that I've been. I've watched miraculous recovery in the financial realm, not only in our lives and our ministry, but ministries all over the world and in individuals as well. We've received some of the most phenomenal testimonies of financial deliverance and miracles that I've ever heard in my life.

The focus of this book is to encourage you to believe God to restore everything the devil has stolen from you. The Lord said to me, "I want you to make a list of everything the devil has stolen from your ministry over the last 5 years and get it back!" So I listed everything Satan had stolen and everything has been restored just like God said. I'm not an isolated case. It will work for whoever will dare believe for it.

Are you fed up with the devil stealing from you? Are you ready to get it back? I want to share with you what the Lord shared with me concerning restoration in every area of our lives.

Behold, the former things are come to pass, and new things do I declare: before they spring forth I tell you of them.

Isaiah 42:9

I want you to make note of the fact that God says, *New things do I declare.* Do you know God is capable of doing something new? Notice that He says, *before they spring forth,* or before they manifest, or before they happen, I will tell you of them. What's God saying? If you don't know what God's doing, then there's a strong possibility that you will miss it.

God said, *My people are destroyed for lack of knowledge.* A vivid example of it is in Luke 5, where Jesus was teaching in a house. The Bible says the place was full of doctors of the law and Pharisees - religious people. And the Bible says, as He taught, the power of the Lord was present to heal them all. Them who? The Pharisees. The doctors of the law. The religious people.

Continue reading and you'll find out that not one of them was healed even though the power of the Lord was present to heal them all. Now somebody did get healed, but it was an outsider. Some men brought a man on a stretcher who couldn't come on his own. When they arrived at this house, they couldn't get in the place because it was packed out.

But they wouldn't take no for an answer. So they found a way. They climbed on top of the house, tore the roof off and lowered the man down. When Jesus saw their faith, the man was healed of his disease. Now notice, there was a whole room full of people that could have been healed but were not because they were not in the flow. That tells me that God can be doing something and not everyone will be affected by it. If you're so preoccupied with your problem, you may not hear the answer.

God said, "I want to do something new and before it springs forth, I tell thee of it." There's a key phrase - *spring forth*. Anything that can *spring forth* can catch you off guard. You've got to be expecting. You've got to be anticipating. God is actually wanting us to get "something new" minded. Go around expecting it. Talking it. Expect something new all the time. Anticipate it. Then when it happens, it won't catch you off guard. You won't be on the outside looking in; you'll be right in the middle of it. Praise God.

Notice He says,

New things do I declare: before they spring forth I tell you of them.

Isaiah 42:9

The Lord shall go forth as a mighty man, he shall stir up jealousy like a man of war: he shall cry, yea, roar; he shall prevail against his enemies.

I have long time holden my peace; I have been still, and refrained myself: now will I cry like a travailing woman; I will destroy and devour at once.

Isaiah 42:13-14

Hear, ye deaf; and look, ye blind, that ye may see.

Who is blind, but my servant? or deaf, as my messenger that I sent? who is blind as he that is perfect, and blind as the Lord's servant?

Seeing many things, but thou observest not; opening the ears, but he heareth not.

Isaiah 42:18-20

He says, the only thing that is preventing me from doing this new thing is, my servants are spiritually blind and spiritually deaf.

Now remember, God says He does nothing in the earth unless He first reveal it.

Surely the Lord God will do nothing, but he revealeth his secret unto his servants the prophets.

Amos 3:7

Isn't that what His Word says? And notice He says, I will do something new, but before I can do it, I have to have somebody listening and seeing. When God gets ready to do something new in the earth, He needs a mouthpiece.

What happens if God's ready to do something but He doesn't have anybody hearing? It's delayed, postponed. God needs listening ears. God needs seeing eyes. In the Old Testament, that's what a prophet was. A seer. A hearer. He saw and he heard what God wanted to do, and God used him as a mouthpiece to declare it to the people. And once the prophet began to decree it, then God had legal right to confirm it with signs following.

It's the same way with you and me. Now you can read in the Word and discover that God wants you to have a certain thing, but it'll never come to pass until you start to decree it.

In Job, it says, *Thou shalt also decree a thing, and it shall be established.* That's a spiritual law. Just because you found it in the Word doesn't mean it's going to happen. It'll happen when you begin to decree it. Because once you begin to decree it, then you've given God the legal right to confirm it with signs following in your behalf.

> *Who is blind, but my servant? or deaf, as my messenger that I sent?*
>
> *Seeing many things, but thou observest not; opening the ears, but he heareth not.*
>
> *This is a people robbed and spoiled; they are all of them snared in holes, and they are hid in prison houses: they are for a prey, and none delivereth; for a spoil, **and none saith, Restore.***
>
> Isaiah 42:19-20,22

Notice the word RESTORE. Highlight it. Underline it. Draw a circle around it. **Restore** was the new thing that he was talking about.

Remember he said, *New things do I declare: before they spring forth I tell you of them.* God is saying, "There's something I want to do and before it comes to pass, I will tell you about it. But if you are going to be a recipient of this new thing, then you've got to have hearing ears."

Do you have ears to hear? I'm not talking about these connected to your head. I'm talking about ears to hear what the spirit of God is saying. If you don't have ears to hear what the spirit of God is saying, then you're going to wind up being robbed and wind up living below your privileges as a child of God.

Once again, God's people are destroyed because of a lack of knowledge. And it's not because God's not giving knowledge. There is an abundance of knowledge. In fact in the book of Proverbs it says, Wisdom is crying out in the streets. God's talking in every way that He possibly can.

We have access to twenty-four hour Christian television, radio programs, magazines and tapes. Now we're even getting the message out on the Internet. There is no excuse for a believer having a lack of knowledge. As Proverbs says, *Ye simple ones, how long, ye simple ones, will ye love simplicity?*

God is saying, "I want to do something new, but I have to have somebody listening so I can tell it to them and then they must decree it. And once they decree it, then it gives Me legal right to do it in their behalf."

Verse 22, *and none saith, Restore.* Then look at verse 23, *Who among you will give ear to this?* What's God saying? I'm ready to do something new. What is this new thing, Lord? "Restoration! I'm ready to restore. I'm ready to restore to you everything the adversary has stolen from you. I'm ready to turn this devastation in your life into restoration, but I must have someone declaring restoration."

What about you? Will you be the person God's looking for? How badly do you need restoration in your life? If you need it, then start decreeing restoration in your home right now!

CHAPTER 4

CHAPTER 4

Changing Your Atmosphere

My oldest grandson, Mark James, is my preaching buddy. This little boy has been preaching with me since he could just barely talk. I think his first words were "Pa Pa" and then "Preaching" was about the second word. He just loves to preach.

I gave him one of my old microphones, and it became one of his favorite toys. He went all over the house with that microphone just preaching when he could hardly even talk. And he loves suits. He thinks suits are for preaching only. When I take him to the department store, he grabs the salesman's coat and says, "Where's your preaching suits?" He thinks that's all they're for.

He would come over to our house in a suit to play. I would say, "Mark James, why do you have your suit on?" "In case we preach, Pa Pa," he'd say. One time he came over in a jogging suit and a tie. I said, "Why do you have on a tie?" "In case we preach, Pa Pa."

Every once in a while I would take him with me on meetings, and he wanted to dress just like me. So I'd get him dressed and I'd say, "Now you just sit there and be real still and don't mess your clothes up. Let me get dressed and the Pastor will be here in a little while to pick us up." I'd say, "Now get your sermon ready." And he'd have his Bible open, even though he couldn't read it, and he'd say, "Pa Pa, are you going to do all the preaching or do I get to preach too?" He'd get upset if I didn't let him preach before I did.

So one morning after a meeting we had in Tulsa, we went to the airport very early to catch a flight back to Dallas/Fort Worth. As we were going through security, Mark James said, "Pa Pa, you didn't give me breakfast, and I'm hungry." I said, "Well there's a little snack bar just before the gate. We'll have enough time to get you something before we get on the airplane." So we stopped at this little snack bar. There was one table left, and so we sat down. There just seemed to be a real nice atmosphere that particular morning.

Airports are notorious for strife, but it just seemed to be real peaceful there. People seemed to be having a good time. I had him sit down, and I went up to the counter. The lady at the counter watches our television program and said hello to me, and I got some orange juice and a muffin for him. We were having a great time.

Well in a little while, two men came walking down the hall telling a dirty joke - very, very loudly. I mean they were speaking the most foul language I'd ever heard in my life. Eventually, everybody in the airport turned their head to look at these guys. They just didn't have any respect for anybody. Filthy words were coming out of their mouths, and they simply did not care who was listening. They came right up to the snack bar, sat down at a table right next to us and continued telling their dirty joke. And my grandson could hear it. He could hear everything they were saying, and he is a very impressionable little boy. He picks up on everything he hears and repeats it.

It made me mad. I mean, I almost forgot who I was and what I was, and I wanted to slap them both real good and then pray for their healing. I mean, it really made me mad. I found out I wasn't totally sanctified that morning. It just got all over me. But I can't slap them. I mean, the lady at the counter knows who I am. If I slap this guy, then what am I going to tell her? "God told me to cast that devil out of him through five fold ministry. Here's five and it's folded." I can't do that.

These two men totally changed the atmosphere in that airport with their filth. I thought, "Now wait a minute. It was nice here before these two 'jerks' showed up. We've got just as much right to enjoy our breakfast here in a peaceful atmosphere." And I came to a solution.

I just said real loud, "Mark James, are you going to help Pa Pa preach tonight when we get to Ft. Worth?"

He said, "I am."

I said, "Have you got your sermon ready?"

He said, "I do."

I said, "Well, I'd like to hear a sample of it."

He does not have any reservations whatsoever. He just thinks you ought to preach everywhere. Here's what he did. He got out of his chair, got in front of the table, looked at everybody in the snack bar and hit the table with his fist. Then he said real loud, "People, you need Jesus in your heart and you need to be filled with the Holy Ghost!"

You could see the shock on those two guys' faces. Their mouths flew wide open and they got up and walked off just as fast as they could.

Then Mark James said, "Say amen, somebody." (He

loves that line from Kenneth Copeland.) And people started clapping for the little guy. A three year old changed the atmosphere in the airport with his words.

Now if he can do that in an aiport, then you can do it in your house. Don't tell me it won't work for you. God said I want to do something new. And this new thing is: He wants to restore everything the devil has stolen. But it's not going to happen to you because it happened to me or because it happened to somebody else. It's going to happen because you get it down on the inside of you to the point that no one can take it away from you. Decree it and keep decreeing it and keep decreeing it and keep decreeing it until comes to pass.

Restoration is not automatic. It's going to happen to you when you hear what I heard. I heard God say, "Son, it is time to get back everything the devil has stolen from you. Start decreeing, Restore! Restore! Restore!" Remember He said, "I don't have anybody saying restore." I read that and I said, "God, I'll be Your man. Everywhere I go. Every city I preach in. Every nation I preach in. I'm going to charge the air with restoration." Hallelujah. That's what you do when you begin to decree it. You charge the atmosphere with restoration. Praise God.

Many years ago when Smith Wigglesworth came to America, he was preaching in a meeting where there was a number of preachers. They asked him to come to the service the night before he was to speak. Brother Wigglesworth was sitting in the audience listening to a man preaching total unbelief and religious tradition. Finally, Brother Wigglesworth couldn't stand it anymore. He just stood up, interrupted the man, and of course, Wigglesworth had a powerful voice and he just shouted, "Stop him, Lord, he's charging the air with unbelief." The man shut up, sat down and Brother Wigglesworth took over and changed the atmosphere by preaching words of faith. Consequently, miracles began to happen.

Notice those words. The first time I read that, that phrase stuck in my spirit. "Charging the air." He's charging the air with unbelief. The Bible says that through faith and understanding God framed the worlds. You frame your own world with the words that you speak. My world is charged with faith, with life, with health, with prosperity, with victory and with success. Why? Because I charge the air with them.

We're in this world, but we're not of this world. We can frame our world with the words of God coming out of our mouth, and God confirming them with signs following. God said I don't have anyone saying "restore". And God says if they'll say it, I'll do it. Do you need restoration happening in your life? Well then begin declaring it and give God an opportunity to do it!

The book of Acts, chapter 3 tells us that heaven retains Jesus until all things have been restored. So if we believe His appearing is soon, then this restoration is even sooner than that. These are days of restoration, praise God. God is restoring. He is restoring back to the church everything that Satan has taken out of the church.

Now you may say, "Well I just don't believe that my going around saying 'Restore' will do anything." All right, let me ask you this, "Have you ever been in a restaurant or some public setting, perhaps you and your family, very comfortable and then people sat next to you and start using foul language?" Did it change the atmosphere? What changed it? Not just their presence, but their words. If it works in the negative, then why not in the positive?

Start charging the air with "Restore"! Husbands, you are the priest and the prophet of your home. You ought to be the family cheerleader. Get them up in the morning and say, "All right family. We are fed up with the devil stealing from us. He has stolen from us for the last time so in the name of Jesus, let's all begin our cheer for the day. Jesus said be of good cheer so here's a good cheer. R-E-S-T-O-R-E! What am I spelling? Restore! Restore! Restore!" Amen. Get them all talking restore.

I heard what God was saying, and I began to decree it and it began to happen, praise God. If the rest of the body of Christ begins decreeing it, then there is no demon in hell that can keep back what has been stolen from us. We are the generation that's going to march in and get it all back. Hallelujah.

Look at II Kings 7:3. You're probably familiar with this story. I want you to see how even though what was in the enemy's camp was available to God's people, it didn't happen until somebody got in motion. It was there all the time. It belonged to them, but they never benefited from it until somebody got in motion.

And there were four leprous men at the entering in of the gate: and they said one to another, Why sit we here until we die?

II Kings 7:3

Notice, these were leprous men. They already had three strikes against them. These men are the least likely to be used of God to restore to a whole community its food and its wealth. The supply lines have been cut off. There is no food in the city. There's no food to be bought. These men are either going to die of leprosy, or they're going to die of starvation, or they're going to die by the sword of the enemy. They have no hope. They know they're going to die one way or the other.

But finally, one of them made up his mind, well if we're going to die, we're not going to just sit here, we're going to die on the move. Why sit we here until we die? Now the question I have for you is: Why sit there when God is saying, "Everything Satan has stolen from you I will restore." Why go without, if God's saying it's time to get it back? Amen.

So they said,

Why sit we here until we die?

If we say, We will enter into the city, then the famine is in the city, and we shall die there: and if we sit still here, we die also. Now therefore come, and let us fall unto the host of the Syrians: if they save us alive, we shall live;

and if they kill us, we shall but die.

2 Kings 7:3-4

In other words, we're not going to just sit here and accept defeat anymore. And they rose up in the twilight to go into the camp of the Syrians.

> *And when these lepers came to the uttermost part of the camp, they went into one tent, and did eat and drink, and carried thence silver, and gold, and raiment, and went and hid it; and came again, and entered into another tent, and carried thence also, and went and hid it.*

2 Kings 7:8

Now if you read the entire story, these four leprous men got up and started toward the enemy's camp. And through their action, it caused a reaction from God. All they did was say, we're not going to sit here anymore and just accept defeat. So they got up and started walking toward the enemy's camp, and God responded. He amplified the sound of their footsteps and caused the Syrians to hear the sound of a mighty army. And all it was, was four leprous men. The Syrians were so afraid by what they heard they didn't even send a scout out. All they'd had to do was send a scout out and they would've seen four leprous, helpless, hopeless men crawling over the hillside. But God amplified that sound and made it sound like a great host, an entire army. And it frightened the enemy so, that they fled the camp.

And when these four leprous men got to the enemy's camp, they found all the food that was needful. They found all the finances that were needful. And it was sitting there waiting for them all the time. But notice, no one would have benefited from it if someone hadn't gotten into motion. Notice how the motion started. Words. *Why sit we here until we die?* It started with words. Right words. When they got there, every tent they went into, they found abundance. And then they finally decided it wouldn't be right for them to consume it on themselves. They told the city what they had found. And the whole city began to rejoice as they took back what the enemy had stolen.

So once again, God is saying, "I'm ready to do something wonderful in your life. I am ready to restore everything the enemy has taken from you. All I need for you to do is have listening ears. Say what I say and decree it and establish it and get in motion."

I'm telling you there is no demon in hell that can hold back or keep back what's been stolen from you if you'll do what God is saying.

Say it right now: Restore! Restore! Restore! Say it again: Restore! Restore! Restore!

It's very important that you don't get the impression that you're going to say it once and that's it. You keep decreeing it. If you'll do what God is saying in Isaiah 42 - become "something new minded," then the last thing you'll say when you go to bed at night is **Restore!** The first thing you'll think when you get up in the morning - **Restore!** When you talk to the family: "These are our days of restoration." When you talk to people on the job, and somebody says, "How's it going?" You'll say, "Restoration, thank you."

Get so "restoration minded" that it just flows out of you. Restore! Restore! Restore! And you just watch, God is going to do something new in your life!

In these last days, God will raise up an army of believers that are going to march into Satan's camp and take back everything he has stolen from the church. Begin charging the air with restoration in your home, get it in your spirit and start shouting, "Restore! Restore! Restore!"

CHAPTER 5

CHAPTER 5

If You Can Conceive It, You Can Receive It

Have you ever wondered, "Can God provide the money that I need to get out of debt?" Or "Can He provide new school clothes for the kids?" Or "Can He provide the finances to pay our rent this month?" Well, every time you question God, you are putting limitations on Him.

Every time you ask, "Can He?" instead of boldly declaring by faith, "He can," you limit God in your life! Even though God is totally unlimited, you and I can limit Him from doing what He wants to do in our lives.

Get the phrase, "Can He?" out of your vocabulary. "Can God do this, can God furnish that, can God provide this?" HE CAN! If you can conceive it, then you can receive it and no demon from hell can keep it out of your possession.

You limit Him by not being able to conceive it in

your heart. Nothing happens on the outside until it is first conceived on the inside! We know that in the natural realm "to conceive" means "to become pregnant with," but it also means "to apprehend." In other words, reach out and take it!

I found a definition of *pregnant* in the dictionary that I did not know before. It means "to be filled with or to be rich in prolific ideas!" I am pregnant with some prolific ideas, and I got them from the Bible. I am conceiving what God says is mine. How about you?

For as he thinketh in his heart, so is he...

Proverbs 23:7

As a man thinks in his heart (not his head). Thinketh in the heart implies, "to ponder, to dwell upon, to meditate, to imagine or to image." You have to be able to conceive the image on the inside of you of what God is saying and what God is promising. If you can't conceive an image of it, then it will never become a reality in your life.

If you still question, "Can He?" then the image is not perfected yet. That means you've got to spend more time with the Word and more time with the

Holy Ghost. Obviously, in order to conceive something, it takes more than just attending church only, it takes more than reading the Bible once a week on the way to church, and more than hearing a sermon one time. Faith cometh by hearing and hearing. Repetition. The more you hear it, the more capable you become of conceiving it.

God is ready to work with a people who will remove every limitation and allow Him to do some big things in their lives. He wants you to stretch your imagination just as far as you can possibly stretch it. In fact, from here on out THINK BIG!

God is telling us that He's going to do some big things (exceeding abundantly above all that we can ask or think) and yet the only ones who are going to experience this are those who can conceive it.

Remember the story of the children of Israel (Psalm 78). God did marvelous things in their behalf (divided the Red Sea in order for them to cross over) and yet they still questioned God saying, "Can God furnish, can God give, can God provide?"

Consequently, people with that outlook will not experience the exceedingly if they can't conceive it. I realize many times, the thing that keeps us from thinking big is the fact that we've had so many trials and so many attacks that all we can think is, "I just want to survive."

If you can't conceive restoration in your life, then you won't experience it. God used this concept to get Abraham to see beyond his own limitations and believe what He had promised.

In Genesis 13, Abram begins his journey of faith. God says to him in verse 15,

For all the land which thou seest, to thee will I give it, and to thy seed for ever.

And I will make thy seed as the dust of the earth: so that if a man can number the dust of the earth, then shall thy seed also be numbered.

Genesis 13:15-16

So God tells him, "Look, as far as you can see in every direction around you, that's what I'm going to give you. Now I want you to look down at the dust. If you can count every little grain of dust, Abram, that's how many seed you will have."

God's talking to a man who, in the natural, has limitations. This can never come to pass. But did you notice, God pays no attention to what man says about Abram's condition (or yours). Notice what He said in verse 17,

> *Arise, walk through the land in the length of it and in the breadth of it; for I will give it unto thee.*
>
> Genesis 13:17

Why does God want Abram to feel the dust on his feet? Because if he can feel the very dust that God says is his, it helps create the image on the inside of his heart. Then, in Chapter 15, in order to continue perfecting this image on the inside of Abram, it says,

> *And he brought him forth abroad, and said, Look now toward heaven, and tell the stars, if thou be able to number them: and he said unto him, So shall thy seed be.*
>
> *And he believed in the Lord..*
>
> Genesis 15:5-6

What is He doing? God is helping Abram conceive an image on the inside. Notice these three words, "And he believed..." You could add, "And he conceived!" However, he had a little problem. His wife was not out there walking in the dust with him. His wife was not out there counting stars. So how can you expect her to conceive what Abram has conceived.

Husbands and wives, you are living this life of faith together. It's not enough for one to conceive restoration, and the other hasn't. It's not enough for me to get an image and Carolyn not have the same image. As long as only one of us has an image of it, we put limitations on ourselves. We're one in this walk of faith.

Abram has an image of it. He has conceived! He believes God. He's pregnant on the inside with the vision. However, it's not that real to Sarai. And when it's not real to your mate, he/she can be easily distracted.

Sarai said, *it may be...* That's unbelief. When you say, "it may be", you haven't conceived yet. Then, God changed Abram's name to Abraham meaning "Father of many nations". Now, every time Sarai calls his name, she's saying, "Father of many nations, it's time to eat now." "Father of many nations, it's time to go to work now."

In order to perfect this image in Sarai, God had to change her name too. Notice what happened,

As for Sarai, thy wife, thou shalt not call her name Sarai, but Sarah shall her name be.

Genesis 17:15

Sarah means "princess or the mother of nations."

And I will bless her, and give thee a son also of her: yea, I will bless her, and she shall be a mother of nations; kings of people shall be of her.

Genesis 17:16

Notice what God has done. He is endeavoring to perfect the image on the inside of them because what they can't conceive, they can't receive. Now every time Sarah hears her name called... "Oh, Sarah!" "Oh, mother of nations, what's for supper?"

Every time they call one another's name, the image gets more and more perfected until they believe beyond a doubt that they can do what God says they can do.

And the Lord visited Sarah as he had said, and the Lord did unto Sarah as he had spoken.

For Sarah conceived...

Genesis 21:1-2

I know this is talking about physically conceiving, but she couldn't physically conceive until she spiritually conceived. In other words, she could not conceive in her womb until she first conceived in her heart. It had to happen in the heart first.

Somebody might ask, "Are you saying confession brings possession?" Yes. What else would you call repeating someone's name all the time? Confession. God had them confessing the promise every time they spoke each other's name.

How much can your spirit conceive? How big can you dream? What kind of restoration do you need in your life? Can you conceive it? What limitations have you placed on God? Are you still asking, "Can He?" You can't just hear a sermon once and think that will do it. It's unlikely that one sermon will cause a perfected image on the inside of you. You've got to walk in the Word on a daily basis from the length of it to the breadth of it. Search out every scripture you can possibly find that talks to you about your situation. Feed on it, imagine it, ponder it, dwell on it, walk in it. Every time you open the Bible, it's not just words, it's life jumping off the pages into your spirit, and you're finally able to shout, "He can!"

I have strength for all things in Christ Who empowers me [I am ready for anything and equal to anything through Him Who infuses inner strength into me; I am self-sufficient in Christ's sufficiency].

Philippians 4:13
(Amplified Bible)

It's time to remove every barrier and every limitation. This can only come from constant fellowship with the Word of God, the Holy Ghost and the Anointed One and His anointing.

Now unto him that is able to do exceeding abundantly above all that we ask or think, according to the power that worketh in us.

Ephesians 3:20

Anytime you see "according to" it means "in direct proportion to." You could say it like this: "Now unto him that is able to do exceeding abundantly above all that we ask or think, in direct proportion to my ability to conceive."

What's he telling us? That this power that is at work within us is a God-given ability to conceive the image of what God says. He will only do exceeding abundantly above what you can ask or think in direct proportion to what you are capable of conceiving.

Now if you can't conceive total restoration, you will never receive it. If you can't conceive increasing in the blessings of God, then you will never experience it because you can only receive what you can conceive.

Begin studying the scriptures until you know that you know without a doubt that nothing is impossible to him who believes. And if you can conceive it, then you can receive what God says is yours! Start shouting, "He Can!"

CHAPTER 6

CHAPTER 6

Staying Positive
in a Negative World

It has become very popular in America for people to tell all of their unfortunate childhood experiences. It's one of the great audience "attention getters" on talk shows today. We've even got psychologists who plant an idea in people's minds, and then the person says, "Oh, that's the reason I can't do this. That's the reason I can't achieve. That's the reason I've been held back all of my life."

Well listen! If you've been abused or mistreated, God has a solution - get born again. "Oh, that's easy for you to say, Brother Jerry. You don't know the pain. You don't know the scars." Let me ask you this? Are you going to let it control you for the rest of your life? You can be healed. You can be delivered. The same Jesus that can heal sick bodies can heal wounded spirits.

It's time to get in the Word of God and tell the devil, "This is where you get off. This will not be a crutch in my life anymore. I don't care what my past was like, my future is bright in God."

Turn all those negative excuses into positive reasons for achieving. The Bible is absolutely full of stories of men and women who were failures but God made champions out of them. Have you ever taken a close look at the "Jesus Christ Evangelistic Association" team? How would you like to have a faith ministry and you have a man on your team known as "Doubting" Thomas? This was a healing ministry and Peter would cut your ear off if you made him mad. This was a ministry of compassion but James and John would call fire down on you. This was a ministry of integrity, and Judas was stealing!

Jesus spent hours one day sharing with His disciples about His relationship with the Father. He made statements such as, "If you've seen Me, you've seen the Father." "My Father and I are One." "It is the Father in Me that doeth the works." And when He got through, Philip said, "Show us the Father." Jesus said, "How long am I going to have to be with you?" Don't laugh, some of his descendants are living all over America. In the natural, these men were the least likely to succeed, but Jesus made new men out of them.

FROM DEVASTATION TO RESTORATION

Who through faith subdued kingdoms, wrought righteousness, obtained promises, stopped the mouths of lions,

Quenched the violence of fire, escaped the edge of the sword, out of weakness were made strong, waxed valiant in fight, turned to flight the armies of the aliens.

Hebrews 11:33-34

These were just ordinary people like you and me who believed God, and their believing God caused them to do extraordinary things. I like what the Message translation says, *...turned disadvantage to advantage.*

This is a negative world that we live in. If you follow the course of this world, then it begins to control your destiny. Satan is endeavoring to plant negative seeds on the inside of you in one way or the other. He is out to restrict you by saying that you're a failure, or you were born on the wrong side of the tracks, or you were born into the wrong family. He'll even tell you that you shouldn't have been born at all.

You can believe that if you want to, or you can overcome it with the Word of God.

Don't become so well adjusted to your culture that you fit into it without even thinking. Instead, fix your attention on God. You'll be changed from the inside out.

Romans 12:1-2
(The Message)

Before anything happens outwardly, something must happen inwardly. *For as he thinketh in his heart, so is he* (Proverbs 23:7).

The Bible won't do any more for you than any other book unless you allow the words to jump off the pages and get into your heart. And that only comes by fellowship and meditation in the Word of God. You'll begin to see yourself as a champion in Christ Jesus, capable of doing all things through the Mighty One which strengthens you.

1. YOU MUST MAKE A DECISION.

Everything you do starts with a decision. Are you going to live like the rest of the world and be controlled by its circumstances or live by the design that God has planned for your life? Success in your life begins with a decision.

FROM DEVASTATION TO RESTORATION

To go with the flow of this world is to live with limitations, but to go with the flow of God is to open yourself to unlimited possibilities never before imagined. Don't allow yourself to join in on negative conversations that are contrary to what you believe.

> *The grass withereth, the flower fadeth: but the word of our God shall stand for ever.*
>
> Isaiah 40:8

It doesn't make any difference what happens in this world; if you are on the Word of God, then you can be a success going somewhere to happen!

> *For I know the thoughts that I think toward you, saith the Lord, thoughts of peace, and not of evil, to give you an expected end.*
>
> Jeremiah 29:11

Make the decision today that you will not allow the world to dictate what your outcome will be. Your outcome is mapped out by God Himself, and your future is bright.

2. LEARN TO THINK BIG.

To flow with God is to open up your mind and think bigger thoughts than you've ever thought in your life. You'll be able to dream new dreams. You'll begin to achieve things that the world says are impossible. You'll begin to believe that you can conquer every obstacle that stands in your path. If God is for you, no one can successfully be against you.

You can't "hang around" God very long and continue to think small. He said to me one time, "If you think small, you will disappoint Me." The Word challenges you to rise above the circumstances of this world, and to get a brand new perspective of your potential in Christ. I'm not talking about what you can do. I'm talking about what the Greater One inside of you can do.

> *So, what do you think? With God on our side like this, how can we lose?*

> Romans 8:37
> (The Message)

3. YOU MUST RENEW YOUR MIND.

> *Be not conformed to this world: but be ye*

transformed by the renewing of your mind, that ye may prove what is that good, and acceptable, and perfect, will of God.

Romans 12:2

Notice the responsibility is on you. God's not going to step in and see to it that you're not conformed. The Holy Ghost isn't going to make you renew your mind. It's up to you. Don't be like the rest of the world.

In February, 1969, when I surrendered my life to God, my whole life changed. I became a new creation. However, nothing happened to my mind! My mind didn't get born again. It was my spirit that got re-created. My mind still thought like it always did. Renewing the mind is not something that happens at the new birth, it is a daily process that begins when you start feeding on the Word of God.

As you saturate yourself in the Word of God, your thinking will begin to change. You'll no longer be a negative person. Just because everybody else talks sickness and poverty doesn't mean that you have to. You may be the only light in that arena of darkness - so shine!

Let me challenge you to do this exercise. It will be a great help to you. Make a list of everything Satan has told you in the past as to why you can't be successful and why you can't be prosperous. For example:

1. Not enough education.
2. Not enough money.
3. Not enough time.
4. Bad childhood experiences.
5. Abused.
6. Born on the wrong side of town.
7. Born to the wrong family.
8. Born at the wrong time.
9. Born at all.

Once you make that list, then compare it to what God's Word says and decide whose report you will believe. Every one of those excuses can be turned into something positive.

What's holding you back? What's keeping you down? Well, it's time to get rid of it.

...let us lay aside every weight, and the sin which doth so easily beset us, and let us run with patience the race that is set before us,

FROM DEVASTATION TO RESTORATION

Looking unto Jesus the author and finisher of our faith.

Hebrews 12:1-2

Study your Bible again. Most of the people in the Bible were not qualified when God called them. They didn't have the credentials. But God takes the foolish things and confounds the wise. God takes what the world discards and turns them into champions, praise God!!

There is a way to stay positive in a negative world by focusing your attention on God. Don't let the world dictate your destiny. Turn every negative excuse into a positive reason for achieving and watch what God will do with your life. He'll turn devastation into restoration!

CHAPTER 7

CHAPTER 7

Delays: Why they Happen & How to Deal With Them

Anyone who has ever attempted to live by faith has experienced delays. I can honestly say, not everything has happened in the time frame I wanted it to or exactly the way I thought it should happen. But I also can say this - God has never disappointed me. There is a due season for everything, and when you understand that, it eliminates the frustration.

There may have been things you were believing for: finances, restoration, job promotion, a godly mate, and it seemed like they would never come to pass, so you finally just gave up. Well, I want to encourage you today to recapture your vision and wait for it until it comes to pass. You may have given up, but God is still interested in seeing His plan come to pass in your life.

When Paul wrote, *Having done all, to stand. Stand,* he indicated that not everything would happen immediately. You must develop "the art of waiting," and I can assure you, I am an expert on this subject.

We generally don't like the scripture that says, *The steps of a good man are ordered by the Lord...* We want it to say, "The strides..." or "The leaps..." Steps are slow, but they are the sure way to go. If you'll determine to obey each step that God gives you, then you will reach the destination that you desire. Let's look at three scriptural reasons for delays:

#1 God. It could be that God has orchestrated a delay in your life because He is arranging a divine appointment up ahead. The illustration I am about to give you is rare. It is not the norm in most Christians lives as to why delays happen, but it can happen.

> *Now when they had gone throughout Phrygia and the region of Galatia, and were forbidden of the Holy Ghost to preach the word in Asia,*
>
> *After they were come to Mysia, they assayed to go into Bithynia: but the Spirit suffered them not.*
>
> Acts 16:6-7

Notice they wanted to preach the Word in Asia,

but they weren't allowed to. Why? The Holy Spirit forbid them. These men, in an attempt to fulfill the commission of Jesus, were delayed in going to Asia and the delay was orchestrated by God. God intervened here because they were about to miss a divine appointment ahead.

> *And a vision appeared to Paul in the night: there stood a man of Macedonia, and prayed him, saying, Come over into Macedonia, and help us.*
>
> *And after he had seen the vision, immediately we endeavored to go into Macedonia, assuredly gathering that the Lord had called us for to preach the gospel unto them.*
>
> Acts 16:9-10

So, God stood between them and their plans and forbid them to preach in Asia because He had another plan up ahead. The timing was not right, and they had a divine appointment awaiting them. This could be the case in your life.

#2 Satan. Delays can be caused because you were hindered by Satan.

But we, brethren, being taken from you for a short time in presence, not in heart, endeavored the more abundantly to see your face with great desire.

Wherefore we would have come unto you, even I Paul, once and again; but Satan hindered us.

1 Thessalonians 2:17-18

Now I can promise you, when you find the word hindered, the source for this delay is not God but Satan. Satan is the one who hinders. That means Satan created this delay. Notice, Paul wanted to come. It was his desire and his intention, but Satan hindered. It could be that Satan has hindered some things in your life and it's time for you to get "fed up" with it and fight back with an aggressive stand on the Word of God.

#3 You. You could be the cause of delays for various reasons. Now obviously, when you create the delay, Satan is behind it, but let's not blame him for everything. In most cases, we need to re-evaluate our lives to see what we've done to create a delay.

Ye have sown much, and bring in little; ye eat, but ye have not enough; ye drink, but ye are not filled with drink; ye clothe you, but there is none warm; and he that earneth wages earneth wages to put it into a bag with holes.

Thus saith the Lord of hosts; Consider your ways.

Haggai 1:6-7

Notice it didn't say, "Consider the devil's ways." It said, "Consider your ways!" It was their ways that had created the delay. Remember, these people were in exile and God delivered them, brought them back to their homeland and their instruction was to re-build the temple that was lying in ruins.

They started out with zeal, inspiration, hope and faith - just like most of us do when God tells us something that He's going to do in our life. They were excited about it, but suddenly, the enemies from the North began to attack them, not only with weapons, but they made fun of them. They mocked them.

Your adversary, the devil, will launch attacks against you, and if that doesn't discourage you, then he'll use messengers to mock you for living by faith. And sometimes they are relatives - people you know, respect and love. If you receive enough mocking and enough attacks, you could lose your focus. Your vision could become blurred, and you could eventually give up before the manifestation comes. **There are three things that cause us to lose our focus:**

#1. Disinterest. You become disinterested in what God said, and of the vision He gave you. Then apathy sets in. You become passive. You yield to the mockery. When you're not interested in what God is saying and doing, then you begin to pursue your own desires and dreams and become self-centered. When that happens, your life becomes unfruitful.

#2. Discouragement. You can get to the point where it looks like what God told you is never going to happen. It becomes too impossible looking. If you look at the ashes of your life too long, Satan will convince you that you cannot build it back. You could become so discouraged that you eventually give up, and again, your life becomes non-productive.

#3. Dissatisfaction. When you become dissatisfied while waiting for your due season, you desperately need a word from God. Haggai means "festive spirit". God sent the prophet, Haggai, to bring joy back to the people so they could build the temple. If there is anything you need when you are disinterested, discouraged, and dissatisfied, it's a word from God. Surround yourself with the Word.

Learn to be the "Haggai" in your house. Jesus said, *"Be of good cheer."* You've got to learn how to become your own best cheerleader! As previously mentioned, men, you are the priest and prophet of your home, and whether you realize it or not, you create the atmosphere. If you're down and discouraged all the time, that will carry over to the rest of the family.

When things are not going well and it looks like it's never going to come to pass, then the family ought to be able to count on you to rally them, praise God. I don't care if all you do is get the family up and say, "OK. It's pep rally time! The devil says it's never going to happen. We've created a few problems for ourselves, but today, we're going to change some things!! Give me a V-I-C-T-O-R-Y!" Create a festive spirit in your home.

Developing the Art of Waiting

A lot of people don't know how to wait. Society has an impatient, do-it-quick, high tech, computerized, push button mentality. We try to bring all that over into Christianity, but there are times when you have to be willing to wait.

This is how to wait properly: Make sure you've done what the Word requires. Remember what Paul said, "Having done all to stand, stand?" Make a check list and be sure you've done all to stand. If you don't understand what *all* is, go read the entire book of Ephesians again. You'll find that avoiding strife is involved in doing all to stand, forgiving people is part of doing all to stand, and giving is part of doing all to stand.

If you are believing for a financial miracle and you haven't planted any seed, then you haven't done all to stand yet. There is no such thing as increase without planting. You may not have any money, but you have prayer time, or you can encourage someone. Seed isn't always money. You can mow someone's lawn and tell them, "That's my seed." Remember: You are never without seed!

When you've done what the Word requires and done all to stand, then you can be confident that God will bring the manifestation. When you know that you know that you are in right standing with God, then your attitude becomes, "Why wouldn't God answer my prayer? He promised that no weapon formed against the righteous shall prosper."

Expectant is a key word in developing the art of waiting. Live each day expecting your due season to come. If it doesn't come today, wake up the next morning expecting it. Don't ever give up — continue to stand and keep on standing until it arrives.

Wait [expectantly] for the Lord, and He will rescue you.

Proverbs 20:22
(The Amplified Bible)

You've got to learn how to scripturally stand, and then whatever it is that you're believing God for will come to pass.

For the vision is yet for an appointed time and it hastens to the end [fulfillment]; It will not deceive or disappoint. Though it tarry, wait [earnestly] for it.

Habakkuk 2:3
(The Amplified Bible)

So don't give up. Don't become disinterested, discouraged or dissatisfied. Wait earnestly for your due season. It will come!

Offended at God?

What's the bottom line for Satan stealing from you? To get you offended at God. To delay your victory.

Why? Because when you're offended at God, you're not in His presence. And if you're not in His presence, then you're not in position for restoration. I've watched it many times, over the years in the lives of many Christians. You never see them anymore. They're not interested in what God's doing anymore. Why? They're offended at God.

If Satan can steal from you and get you offended at God, then he doesn't have to repay because you're not in God's presence. **It's only in His presence that times of refreshing come.**

When the times of refreshing shall come from the presence of the Lord;

And he shall send Jesus Christ, which before was preached unto you.

Acts 3:19-20

Do you need to read that again? **It's only in His presence that restoration comes.**

"I don't understand. Just about the time I think I'm getting my life in order, this has to happen." Don't get offended at God.

Do you want back what's been stolen, or not? Then don't get offended at God when the devil's stealing from you. If you finish reading this book and tomorrow morning Satan steals something else, the worst thing you can do is to get offended at God, offended at His Word, or get offended at the messenger who brought you the Word. Most people either get mad at God, the message, or the person that preached it. And what you ought to be doing is getting mad at the devil; he's the thief not God.

For I know the thoughts that I think toward you, saith the Lord, thoughts of peace, and not of evil, to give you an expected end.

Jeremiah 29:11

Other translations say, *a future and a hope.* He's talking to people who are in captivity. If you're in captivity financially or physically, God says, even while you're in captivity, My thoughts about you are for a future and a hope. "I have thoughts that I think about you and they are not thoughts of you spending the rest of your life in captivity. My thoughts about

you are returning you to where you belong."
(Author's paraphrase).

*Then shall ye call upon me, and ye shall go
and pray unto me, and I will hearken unto*

you. And ye shall seek me"...

Jeremiah 29:12-13

Do you know how difficult it is to seek God with
all your heart when you're in captivity? When you're
being stolen from?

That's not what human nature wants to do.
Human nature wants to pout, have a pity party, and
get mad at God. But God is saying, "If you want My
thoughts for you to come to pass, then while you're in
captivity, while you're being stolen from, while
you're living beneath your covenant rights, call on Me.
Seek Me. Find Me. Search for Me with all your heart."

I studied this out from original Hebrew and the
indication here is this: **searching** is "with an intensity beyond the norm". The worst thing you can do
when Satan is stealing from you is less praying, less
giving, less fellowshipping with God. And isn't that
what usually happens? Satan steals from you, and the

first thing you want to do is quit going to church, quit giving, quit praying. No, God says when you're in captivity, that's when you turn the intensity up. That's when you turn the volume up on your seeking Him.

Why? Because God says, "Don't get out of My presence. Because if you get out of My presence, you've fallen into the adversary's trap. He won't have to pay it back. He keeps what he stole from you. But if in the midst of that captivity (I don't care how badly you feel about it) keep seeking Me, and I will restore you, Hallelujah."

So let me just encourage you and challenge you today. Whatever has been stolen from you, you can get it back - and then some. Don't get offended at God. It will delay your restoration. Release all offenses and start seeking God with your whole heart. Your due season, your miracle and your breakthrough will come.

CHAPTER 8

CHAPTER 8

In Every Great Storm
There Is a Great Victory

Have you ever gotten out of bed one morning with a smile on your face, feeling great, looking forward to the day ahead and **suddenly** all of Satan's power comes against you? Or you're driving down the freeway, your car is running great and **suddenly** everything falls out from under it?

Have you ever been in a situation like that where a storm arises out of nowhere? Taxes have increased. Electric bill went up. The car unexpectedly broke down. That's the way the devil operates. He loves to catch you off guard. He is hoping that this unexpected attack will cause you to panic, and you'll be unprepared to deal with it. When people panic, they often throw all their Bible lessons out the window, and they respond in fear rather than in faith.

We see an example of this in Mark 4 of Jesus teaching His disciples a parable of how the Kingdom of God operates.

Know ye not this parable? And how then will ye know all parables?

The sower soweth the word.

And these are they by the way side, where the word is sown; but when they have heard, Satan cometh immediately, and taketh away the word that was sown in their hearts.

And when they were alone, he expounded all things to his disciples.

Mark 4:13-15,34

Here Jesus has taken His disciples aside and revealed to them the principles of sowing and reaping. He explicitly said that once the Word is sown, Satan will come immediately to take it away; therefore, we must be on guard at all times to resist his attacks. If anyone should have a revelation of this principle, it should be the disciples, right? I mean, Jesus Himself has just expounded all things to them.

Notice what happens:

And the same day, when the even was come, he saith unto them, Let us pass over unto the other side.

FROM DEVASTATION TO RESTORATION

And there arose a great storm of wind, and the waves beat into the ship, so that it was now full.

Mark 4:35, 37

Now, when Jesus said, *Let us pass over unto the other side,* there was not a cloud in the sky. There was not even a forecast of a storm coming. *And there arose a great storm.* The literal Greek meaning for the word *arose* is "unexpected". They had no idea a storm was coming. This thing came out of nowhere.

In the Greek, the word *great* comes from the word *MEGA* meaning "enormous, huge, overwhelming". In other words, this storm was designed by the forces of hell to destroy them. It's MEGA. The Amplified Bible says, *A furious storm of wind [of hurricane proportions] arose.*

This is not just a little wind blowing. It's so great and severe that it's beating against the ship, water is coming into the boat and these men are frightened. Peter, James and John are fishermen. They've been on water all their lives, but evidently this storm is so bad that it causes fear to arise on the inside of them. And when fear arose, they forgot everything they had been taught. Exactly what Satan was hoping!

I've learned that Satan loves to catch us off guard particularly right after a major victory in our life. Why? Because there's a tendency to drop your guard spiritually after a victory. When you've been believing God for six months for something and you finally win, there's a tendency to want to take all that armour off and throw it in the closet and hope you won't have to use your faith for at least another six months.

While you're enjoying your victory, the devil is scheming and plotting another attack. After every victory, I say, "Hallelujah!" and stand guard! Don't dare take your shield of faith off. Don't dare throw your sword down! Be on guard!

Now, Jesus fully intended for those men to get Him to the other side. It didn't matter if the weather was clear or a storm was raging, He wanted them to take the Word and get Him to the other side! But, the disciples panicked.

> *...And he* (Jesus) *was in the hinder part of the ship, asleep on a pillow: and they awake him, and say unto him, Master, carest thou not that we perish?*

> Mark 4:38

They were so frightened to the point that they thought Jesus didn't care. That is exactly what the devil will try to tell you. He'll even send some nice Christian to tell you, "Well, if this faith stuff works, where's God when you need Him?" If anybody cares about your livelihood, it's Jesus, and He will not forsake you.

The fact that Jesus was asleep in the ship during a MEGA storm indicates to me that as far as He is concerned, everything is under control. It may not look like it in the natural, but it's under control.

You and I have experienced situations like this, not necessarily out on the sea, but that's the way it seems when Satan attacks your finances, your family, your business, your church. Sometimes the attacks come in hurricane proportions and you're thinking, "Dear God, what did I do? What brought this on?"

Have you ever unexpectedly had a need for thousands of dollars before the end of the week? I have, and in the natural, it's not comfortable. But God came through with a tremendous miracle!

You may have marked your calendar one year in advance to be at a certain Believers' Convention and all of hell's powers break loose the week before you are to leave. Satan will try his best to keep you from getting to that meeting. Did you ever notice how the family gets in a fight just before the airplane takes off, or the car breaks down just before you get out of town and it had been working fine?

Isn't it amazing that Jesus was **sleeping** during this mega storm! This ship is being tossed to and fro, there's water in the boat, surely it's splashing over on Jesus, but He's still asleep. They had to wake Him up.

When was the last time you slept through a storm? I'm talking about everything broke loose in your life, and yet you go to bed with the peace of God, wake up with the joy of the Lord, and somebody says to you, "Wow! Wasn't that an awful storm!" And you say, "Did we have a storm?"

That's the way Jesus treated it, and He expected His disciples to use the Word and combat this unexpected storm. Notice what the next powerful line says: ... **AND HE AROSE.** The same Greek word as the first arose: **the storm arose unexpectedly, and Jesus arose unexpectedly!** Satan didn't plan on that.

In the mega storms of life, the devil is not counting on Jesus getting you out of this storm. Just as unexpectedly as this storm arose in your life, Jesus will unexpectedly rise up to counter it, Hallelujah!

All Jesus has to do is REBUKE the storm. The Bible says at His rebuke, mountains melt.

> *And he arose, and rebuked the wind, and said unto the sea, peace, be still. And the wind ceased, and there was a great calm.*
>
> Mark 4:39

Same Greek word "MEGA" is used here to describe the calm that came.

> *And He arose and rebuked the wind and said to the sea, Hush now! That's all it took! ...and the wind ceased (sank to rest as if exhausted by its beating) and there was [immediately] (suddenly) a great calm (a perfect peacefulness).*
>
> Mark 4:39
> (The Amplified Bible)

All it took to defeat this unexpected mega storm of hurricane proportions was the rebuke from the Word of God.

I want you to know that if you're in a storm today and your ship is being tossed to and fro, and it looks like there is no way that you could possibly endure it any longer, the Captain of your salvation has not jumped ship! He's still in your ship, and He's got it fully under control!

I know what I'm talking about, I've been there! God wants you to get out of this "survival mentality" where you just hope, if anything, you come out of the storm alive. That's not God's best for your life. It's time for you to think bigger than you've ever thought before. Expect God to move on your behalf. Expect mega miracles in your life.

From Nothing to Mega

In Luke 5, we read of Peter, James and John who are in the fishing business. They had been out fishing all night, they've been on the boat for hours and haven't caught a single fish. They have nothing to show for all their hours out on the water.

But notice what happens when Jesus came on the scene.

Launch out into the deep, and let down your nets for a draught.

FROM DEVASTATION TO RESTORATION

And Simon answering said unto him, Master, we have toiled all the night, and have taken nothing: nevertheless at thy word I will let down the net.

And when they had this done, they inclosed a great multitude of fishes: and their net brake.

Luke 5:4-6

In other words, a few hours ago they had nothing, now they have MEGA. One moment you have absolutely nothing in your bank account and suddenly you have MEGA. Could you handle that?

You've been believing God, tithing, giving and SUDDENLY, even though it has been months, the financial breakthrough comes. One moment you had nothing and the next moment you have more than enough. That's the God we serve. He can take you from nothing to mega.

I want you to notice what Jesus told Peter to do: *let down your nets...* But what did Peter really do? He let down THE net. What am I saying? Peter didn't fully obey. Even though Jesus blessed him, just think how much more would have been taken if he'd fully obeyed.

God gave mega miracles to a man who had nothing. God is taking faithful people who seem to have nothing and giving them mega! If you've been faithful, your due season is coming!

I don't know what kind of storm you may have experienced in the last few days, weeks, or months, but Jesus is in your ship, the Word of God is in your heart and if you'll dare stand on it, then God is capable of bringing a mega calm into your life.

If you've been waking up in the morning thinking, "Dear God, I can't face another day, this is too overwhelming," if you'll keep standing on the Word of God, then this unexpected storm will turn around and become the greatest victory you've ever experienced!

In every overwhelming experience you're facing, don't give up, don't quit, and don't get discouraged! It's time to pick yourself up, rebuke Satan and declare that there is coming a great, MEGA calm in your life in Jesus' Name! Remember this: Out of a MEGA storm comes a MEGA calm!

You have to ask yourself, "Am I willing to wait for it?" As devastating as the attack is, as overwhelming as the attack is, God can turn the thing around and cause

the blessing to equally overwhelm you, praise God!!
To the point where it is beyond anything you had
expected.

Even though from time to time there may be some
unexpected storms in your life, if you won't give up...
if you won't faint... if you won't "throw in the towel,"
then God will bring a great victory and the overwhelming calm will equal the overwhelming attack.

God's answer to great battles is great victories!
God's answer to great financial attacks is great financial miracles or "mega bucks"! I wrote this down in
my notes: If this will work on wind, then it has to
work on dollars. If out of a great storm can come a
great calm, then out of a great financial attack, can
come a great financial miracle!!! In fact, if you are in a
financial attack right now and it is so overwhelming
and so devastating, then you know as well as I do, if
you are going to be delivered from that attack, then
it's going to have to be BIG!

If you're saying, "This is the greatest financial
attack I've ever had," then what you're saying is, the
miracle you are headed for is going to be the greatest
financial miracle you have ever experienced!! I mean,
you can't have something less than the attack! It's got
to be equal to or greater than the attack. And I've got

news for you. Jesus is standing up in your ship right now joining with you when you stand in faith. He's rebuking the wind right along with you, and He's calling for a great calm. A mega victory!!

God wants us to believe Him for mega results. This is a time of increase, but it must start in your own thinking. If you're going to experience increase outwardly, you're going to have to experience it inwardly first of all. You're going to have to change your thinking where increase is concerned. You're going to have to think bigger than ever before.

Don't limit God by thinking in terms of just barely getting by. Don't limit God by saying, "I just hope to survive this." No, get out of that survival mode and get into increase mode. The Great Provider is in your ship, and He wants to bring mega miracles into your life.

Great is our Lord, and of great power.

Psalm 147:5

Your problem is not greater than God. Your attack is not greater than God. Sometimes it may look that way. Sometimes it looks like it's bigger than what God is capable of doing, but it's not.

FROM DEVASTATION TO RESTORATION

Cast not away therefore your confidence, which hath great recompence of reward.

Hebrews 10:35

God promises mega rewards are in store for those who will not cast away their faith while they are under pressure. As great as your problem may be, it can never be greater than the Greater One who resides on the inside of you.

Greater is he that is in you, than he that is in the world.
I John 4:4

So it's up to you. You must become mega-minded. You must become restoration minded. You must become "greater is He that is in me than he that is in the world" minded.

Once again, if you are in a mega storm right now, and your finances are under attack, your household is under attack, your family is under attack and the thing is so overwhelming that it looks absolutely impossible to overcome, then remember that the Greater One is on the inside of you, and He always arises when great storms arise.

You are not helpless, you are not hopeless and it is not over. In fact, what you are headed for is a mega victory in your life. If this storm is so great that it has you up all night, unable to sleep, just get ready! You're going to spend some nights not able to sleep because of all the blessings and the miracles that have come on you!!! Instead of laying there thinking, "What in the world am I going to do to get out of this?" You're going to be laying there all night praising God for how He got you out of it!! God will turn the captivity!

There's a mega calm for every mega storm!

CHAPTER 9

CHAPTER 9

Develop a
Restoration Mentality

These are times of restoration. You're entitled to it. It belongs to you. Financial restoration is not just so you can hoard it up, but it's for the preaching and the proclaiming of the Gospel. God's looking to us to get this Gospel to the world and bring Jesus back. And we can't do it broke.

> *Repent ye therefore, and be converted, that your sins may be blotted out, when the times of refreshing shall come from the presence of the Lord.*
>
> Acts 3:19

Notice, it's "times" of refreshing and not a "time" singular. If it had said a time of refreshing, then that would indicate that it may be one singular event on God's timetable, and it could have already come and gone, and we may not have gotten in on it. But it says times of refreshing plural. So that means it could happen more than once.

The first time of refreshing that you ever experienced was when your spirit was recreated through making Jesus the Lord of your life. And that made you a candidate for **times** of refreshing thereafter, hallelujah. It can happen frequently. Notice that these times of refreshing come <u>from the presence of the Lord.</u> Notice the source. Notice where they're happening. If you're going to get in on it, you've got to be where it's happening. If you're not in the presence of God, then you're not a candidate for a time of refreshing.

So let me encourage you to stay in His presence. Don't miss it. No matter what the devil does or what he's stolen. No matter how much pressure you're under. Regardless of your circumstances. Don't dare get out of the presence of God because that's where the refreshing comes from. You've got to be in position to receive.

> *When the times of refreshing shall come from the presence of the Lord;*
>
> *And he shall send Jesus Christ, which before was preached unto you:*
>
> *Whom the heaven must receive.*

Acts 3:19-21

Now where you see the word "receive", let me suggest that you write in your margin another word that will give you a better understanding of what he's saying: the word *retain*. You'll find this word in most other translations. Using the word "retain" it would read this way, "Whom the heaven must retain until..." In other words, heaven will not release Jesus until something takes place in the earth.

Now obviously, God's Word has to be fulfilled. The Word said that in the fullness of time, God sent His Son. In other words, He couldn't come until the designated moment...until everything leading up to it had been fulfilled. So God is saying here that there are certain things, certain events, that must take place on planet earth before Jesus can make His appearance for the catching away of the saints.

Heaven will not release Him until these things happen. Now, I realize it's not uncommon to hear people say quite frequently, "The Lord could come tonight." Or, "The Lord may be here tomorrow." Now I'm anticipating it, and I look forward to it. But for now, heaven is retaining Him.

There are still a few things that have to happen. What are they? "Whom the heaven must retain until the times of restitution." I want to put this in terminology that we would use more commonly: Restoration. If it will help you, instead of the word "restitution", insert the word "restoration" - it means the same thing.

> *Whom the heaven must [retain] until the times of [restoration] of all things, which God hath spoken by the mouth of all his holy prophets since the world began.*

> Acts 3:21

What's God saying? I will not release my Son until the times of restoration have been fulfilled. God said, "I am going to restore everything I said I would restore out of the mouth of my prophets."

I don't know what that does for you, but immediately, I start searching through the Word of God to find out what the prophets said God would do. What kind of restoration will He do? What is He going to restore? Because God said that He will restore everything the prophets of old said He would restore, and when He's done it, then heaven will release Jesus and we're out of here, hallelujah.

This time of restoration precedes His appearing. If we all believe that His appearing is near, then times of restoration must be nearer than that. I submit to you that we are right in the middle of it. I like to say it this way, "Restoration is in the air." All you've got to do is get in position to receive.

Now let's go back to one of the most significant verses in the Old Testament concerning restoration. This is so good you're going to be glad you read it.

And I will restore to you the years...

Joel 2:25

Underline *the years.* That's the reason the Lord told me in that visitation to go back and list everything the devil had stolen from our ministry over the last five years.

What's God saying? I want to restore years that have been stolen from you. Now, be honest. Has the devil stolen anything from you over the last five years? Do you want it back? Are you entitled to it? Yes, you are! Let that just sink down into your spirit. Everything the devil has stolen from you. I'm not saying you're limited to five years, that's just what the Spirit of God said to me. You can make this retroactive as far back as your faith will allow. Believe God for everything Satan's stolen from you.

Verse 26 says, *And ye shall eat in plenty.* Notice your condition immediately after restoration. When God restores what the enemy has stolen for years, notice how your lifestyle changes immediately. You shall eat in plenty. Plenty is the nature of God. That's been His plan for you and me since the beginning. It never was the plan of God that we live in the land of "not enough" nor the land of "just enough," but God has always intended for us to live in the land of "more than enough." Amen.

> *And ye shall eat in plenty, and be satisfied, and praise the name of the Lord your God, that hath dealt wondrously with you: and my people shall never be ashamed.*

> Joel 2:26

Three primary reasons why you will never experience shame again.

1) He will restore the years
2) You will experience plenty
3) He will deal wondrously with you

I challenge you to do a word study, particularly in the Psalms. Go find out every time the Psalmist talked about the wonders of God and see how drastically your life will change. He wants to deal wondrously with **you.**

Have you ever lived under the shame of not being able to pay your bills? Have you ever lived under the shame of not being able to do for God what you want to do? Don't you hate that? You're in a meeting or at church and they're ready to add another wing onto the building, it's time to expand, and they need a certain amount of money. And you're sitting there, your heart's just racing and you're thinking, "Dear God, I wish I was in a position to do something bigger than I've ever done before. I'm so tired of just giving fifty dollars. I want to give fifty thousand." Wouldn't that be wonderful!

But notice, he says, *"My people shall never be ashamed."* The shame of not being able to do for your family like you really want to. The shame of not being able to provide for them. And then the shame of not being able to get involved in the needs of others. After a while, you just feel terrible when you can't do something that you really want to do because you're limited and restricted. God said, "When I restore the years, you shall eat in plenty. You'll be satisfied. I'll deal wondrously with you, and you'll never know shame again," hallelujah.

And ye shall know that I am in the midst of Israel, and that I am the Lord your God, and none else: and my people shall never be ashamed.

Joel 2:27

That's very important to God or He wouldn't repeat it twice. Remember what He told Joshua? Before he took him into the promised land, he said, "Today I will roll away the reproach of Egypt from off you."

That's important to God. What was He talking about? To the Israelites, Egypt represented the land of not enough. When they lived in Egypt, they were under taskmasters. They were slaves, and they could never build enough bricks. They could never find enough straw. They could never satisfy the Egyptians enough. So, in the mind of an Israelite, Egypt was the land of not enough. And God said, "I'm going to roll that reproach off of you. You will never live in the land of not enough again. You are headed for a land that flows with milk and honey."

Egypt is a type of the bondage of Satan in which we were held captive. Just like the children of Israel, we have been delivered and we've been brought out - all the chains that bound us have been broken.

Giving thanks unto the Father, which hath made us meet to be partakers of the inheritance of the saints in light:

Who hath delivered us from the power of darkness, and hath translated us into the kingdom of his dear Son.

Colossians 1:12-13

Even though God had brought them out of Egypt, **Egypt was not out of them.**

So Moses brought Israel from the Red sea, and they went out into the wilderness of Shur; and they went three days in the wilderness, and found no water.

And when they came to Marah, they could not drink of the waters of Marah, for they were bitter...

And the people murmured against Moses, saying, What shall we drink?

And he cried unto the Lord; and the Lord showed him a tree, which when he had cast into the waters, the waters were made sweet...

Exodus 15:22-25

God was endeavoring to remove from them every remembrance of their lives in Egypt but they would not let Egypt go.

...And the whole congregation of the children of Israel murmured against Moses and Aaron in the wilderness:

And the children of Israel said unto them, Would to God we had died by the hand of the Lord in the land of Egypt, when we sat by the flesh pots, and when we did eat bread to the full; for ye have brought us forth into this wilderness, to kill this whole assembly with hunger.

Exodus 16:2-3

Every time they faced adversity, they wanted to run back to Egypt. For 40 years they were out of Egypt, but Egypt wasn't out of them.

Forty years long was I grieved with this generation, and said, It is a people that do err in their heart, and they have not known my ways.

Psalms 95:10

It's the same with many Christians today, and until they get "Egypt" out of them, they'll never enter into the land (lifestyle) that God promised. You will never enter into <u>what is to come</u> until you first let go of <u>what has been.</u>

...this one thing I do, forgetting those things which are behind, and reaching forth unto those things which are before.

Philippians 3:13

Remove everything that holds you to your past. Moses took off the garments of Pharaoh's house and "refused to be called the son of Pharaoh's daughter." Bartimaeus took off the garments of a beggar when he met Jesus signifying that all ties to his past had been removed.

You can't drag your past around with you and expect to enter into God's destiny for your life. Tell the devil, "I refuse to be a product of this world. I cast off the garments of my past, in Jesus' Name."

Many people have a "poverty mentality" and it limits God from bringing restoration into their lives. Perhaps your family was poor and that spirit of poverty was passed down to you. Well, take a stand, get right in the devil's face and tell him, "Poverty stops here! I'm entitled to supernatural increase and restoration in Jesus' Name!"

Get that "Egypt mentality" out of your heart and mind and start seeing restoration in every area of your life. It's time to develop a restoration mentality!

CHAPTER 10

CHAPTER 10

God's Way of Restoration

B efore going into the ministry, I was in the automotive business, and my job was repairing wrecked automobiles and restoring antique cars. I owned "Jerry's Paint and Body Shop."

My dad was a paint and body man. He worked for various dealerships in the city where I grew up. From the time I was five years old, my dad took me to the shop where he worked, sat me on a Coke box, and I watched him work on cars. That's all I ever wanted to do. I loved cars, especially old cars, especially fast cars... actually any car. I didn't even care what it was. Cars were my life. I can remember dreaming every night about all the cars that I was going to build.

So when God talks about restoration, I can identify with that. The dictionary says *restore* means: **to bring back to a former or original condition.** The greatest compliment anybody could ever give me when I was in the automotive business was when they came to pick up their car, and as they paid me for my services, they would say, "Jerry, I can't even tell where it was wrecked."

It was brought back to a former or original condition. I took great pride in that because my Daddy taught me the right way to restore automobiles. My dad told me, "If you're not going to do it right, then I'm not going to teach you. If you're going to look for shortcuts, and get paid as soon as you can, then I'm not going to teach you the trade." He said, "My reputation is at stake, and you're not going to ruin it." So, I was taught by the best. When people came to my shop, and they drove that car out telling me, "I can't even tell where it was wrecked," then what they were saying was, "Thank you for restoration according to Webster's Dictionary."

However, I discovered that **God's definition of restoration** is not the same as Mr. Webster. Are you ready for this? Mr. Webster says **restore - to bring back to a former or original condition.** God's definition of **restore - to make better, improve, increase, and multiply.**

If Satan steals something from you, God's idea of restoration is not just to bring you back to former condition, but He's going to make the devil pay, and you're going to wind up improved, better, increased and multiplied, hallelujah.

Let me prove God's definition of restoration to you. We discussed earlier the children of Israel coming out of Egypt (Exodus 12:35). In Egypt, they had taskmasters. They worked ungodly hours. Their task was beyond what you would call the norm. It was non-stop. The Egyptians used Israelites as slaves and took advantage of them.

But notice what God does before He takes them out of Egypt. He compensates. Let me just say this to you. If you've been taken advantage of, if you've worked your fingers to the bone for somebody else and they got rich off of you, don't you dare give up because God's keeping books. Compensation is a part of God's agenda.

Don't get envious of the sinner who's wealthy and you're saying, "Here I am. I go to church. I pay my tithes. I'm just barely skimming by, and look at that guy down the road." Don't get envious of him. The Bible says his prosperity is temporary. It won't last forever, and God rewards the faithful, hallelujah. Here's an example of God's restoration.

And the children of Israel did according to

the word of Moses; and they borrowed of the Egyptians jewels of silver, and jewels of gold, and raiment:

And the Lord gave the people favour in the sight of the Egyptians, so that they lent unto them such things as they required. And they spoiled the Egyptians.

Exodus 12:35-36

One other translation says, *"plundered."* Now get the picture. Pharaoh's sitting on his throne watching nearly 3 million people pass by and not one of them is passing by without silver and gold in his hand.

What's happening? Everything that had been stolen from God's people for 430 years, God saw to it that when they walked out of there, they didn't walk out poor. They didn't barely skim by. They carried everything that should have been theirs in the first place. God got it back and more, hallelujah. Much more! The wealth of the sinner has been laid up for the just. Glory to God.

Go study David and you'll find out the same thing. Even though David didn't build the first temple, he was responsible for raising the funds for it. David, out of his own personal treasury, gave millions toward the building of the temple. The people gave millions for the building of the temple. Where did they get all this money?

Every time he defeated some king, before he left that king's land, he took the king's treasury and brought it back home. And what happened? The wealth of the sinner built the first temple.

I'm telling you, when God restores, you wind up better than before. Improved...Increased...Multiplied, hallelujah. God said He delivered them with a high hand.

I want you to see restoration God's way even under the law of Moses... not Webster's Dictionary. If anyone stole something, God had a restoration program.

> *If a man shall steal an ox, or a sheep, and kill it, or sell it, he shall restore five oxen for an ox, and four sheep for a sheep.*

> Exodus 22:1

Webster's restoration would have been: if someone steals an ox from you or a sheep from you, restore one sheep and one ox back to original, former condition. Not God. God says, "Oh yes, I'll restore, but when it's all said and done, you'll come out better, improved, increased and multiplied."

You know what that tells me? <u>God promises you a return on everything you give, and He promises a return on everything that's been stolen from you.</u> You cannot lose. Either way you come out better...improved...increased... multiplied. Now look at what the devil's been getting away with. The devil steals off of us, and we just cry for about a month, have a pity party, and then let him get away with it.

Then some of us get a little stirred up because we hear a sermon, and we think, "I'm coming at you, devil." But then we get tired. We finally just say, "Oh, forget it." One time, I was so desperate, I said, "God, I'm in a bind here, do You understand? Forget the hundred fold return. Just match me dollar for dollar. I mean, I could pay my bills if You'd just match me dollar for dollar for what I've given. We'll deal with the hundred fold later." Well, that's not God's kind of restoration.

God restores, and you don't come back to original condition. God's restoration program is to your favor. That's the reason God wants us to get stirred up about this. You know what He wants us to do? Break Satan's bank. Get it all back. And it's happening. It is happening all over the world. Satan can't hang onto his stuff anymore because it never really belonged to him in the first place.

Men do not despise a thief, if he steal to satis-
fy his soul when he is hungry.

Proverbs 6:30

The devil could care less what you've been through to get what you've got. Particularly, if you got it by faith.

He's stealing off of God's kids every moment of the day, and a lot of them haven't done a thing about it. They feel badly, get offended at God, and quit going to church. When what we ought to do is get mad at the devil and tell him, "All right. If you steal one of my ox, buster, you're going to bring back five! You understand? I'm going to hold you to this. You're not getting away with this for another second." Finally, he'll get to where when he passes your house, he has second thoughts about stopping because you've beat his brains out with the Word of God every time he steals something off of you.

Men do not despise a thief, if he steal to satis-
fy his soul when he is hungry;

But if he be found, he shall restore sevenfold;
he shall give all the substance of his house.

Proverbs 6:30-31

God said don't despise him if he stole to satisfy his hunger, **but** if he be found, your outcome will be better, improved, increased and multiplied.

If our judiciary system acted on this verse today, we'd have less thieves. What if the law made them pay it back seven fold and hold them to it until they did it? "All right, you stole a car from that family, you're going to repay them seven cars." There would not be as much stealing going on.

Well, what if he doesn't have seven fold? Then he'll give all the substance of his house. If he can't come up with seven fold, then you take everything he's got. I like the sound of this because Satan's a thief, and I found him. I'm not ignorant of his devices. I know who's stealing from me. It's the devil. He's a thief, and if he be found, make him pay seven fold.

Every time you see something being stolen from one of God's people, God gets involved immediately in restoration. But He doesn't bring them back to original condition, He makes them better. That's where we are, folks. We are in days of restoration. God says I can make your life better. Improve it. Increase it. Multiply it.

There's no need in shedding any more tears over what the devil's stolen because it is about to come back, if you'll demand it. If you'll hold his feet to the fire, and you get fed up with him keeping what belongs to you.

God Will Turn Your Captivity

You know the story of Job. Everything the man owned was destroyed, consumed, stolen, devoured. Everything. The Bible said he was the richest man in all the East, and then the thief came.

But when God got through with him...Notice Job 42:10, *And the Lord turned the captivity of Job.* I found from the original Hebrew that means, "put a stop to all the evil." When God turns captivity, as He did with Job, you never see Satan consuming, destroying, devouring anything of Job's ever again. The Lord turned the captivity of Job when he prayed for his friends.

Also, the Lord gave Job twice as much. If God had read Webster's definition, He would have brought Job back to his original condition. But God's restoration program is to make better, improve, increase and multiply. Look at Job's original condition.

His substance also was seven thousand sheep, and three thousand camels, and five hundred yoke of oxen, and five hundred she asses, and a very great household; so that this man was the greatest [or as some other translations say wealthiest] *of all the men of the east.*

Job 1:3

That's original condition. Not bad. The man's living well. He's got it made. And then Satan consumes, destroys, and devours everything. But then God begins His restoration program with Job. And notice, when God restored, He didn't take Job back to original condition. Had He done that, it would violate the very nature of God.

There are a lot of people who would be satisfied to be brought back to original condition. But that's not God's way. God's extravagant. He can't help Himself. Everything He does is big. He's not wasteful, but He's extravagant.

God says, "You stole from one of My kids? Then it's time for restoration." (Author's paraphrase).

So the Lord blessed the latter end of Job more than his beginning: for he had fourteen thousand sheep, and six thousand camels, and a thousand yoke of oxen, and a thousand she asses.

Job 42:12

Job was more blessed in his latter days than in his beginning.

Now he has 14,000 sheep, 6,000 camels, 1,000 yoke of oxen, 1,000 she asses. Exactly doubled. "Yeah, but Brother Jerry, it took a lifetime to get it." No, it didn't. Forty-two chapters of Job does not cover his life, it covers nine to twelve months out of Job's life. That's not his whole life in that book. A lot of people read it, and they think, "Oh, dear God, look what this man went through in his lifetime." No, most theologians agree it was between 9 and 12 months.

It's the worst nine months you ever read about, but keep reading because it turns out to be the best nine months you ever read about. A man is the wealthiest man in all the East, he loves God, he's in right standing with God, serves God and then the enemy comes in and destroys everything he has. But when God got through restoring him, he's not just the wealthiest man in the East, there's nobody even close to him, praise God. I like God's way of restoring. It can happen in your life, too — if you'll dare believe it and start declaring it.

CHAPTER 11

CHAPTER 11

Changing Your Outlook

I trust that this book will be a morale booster and at the same time will create a stirring on the inside of you to never allow Satan to steal anything else from you again.

If you feel as though your life has been overwhelmed by adversity, and you feel as though you've been under the gun, so-to-speak, and you don't know where to turn, you don't know what to do, you're devastated in some way, then you are a candidate for a time of refreshing.

Anybody can dance and shout in church, but where your faith really counts is when all of hell's power has broken loose against you at home. We can't all go home with you every time you come under attack. So, you better learn to stay full of faith all the time.

It's not likely that Satan's going to attack you in

church. He's going to wait until you get home, and make you think that all you heard really doesn't work.

It's not likely that you will see people have pity parties and stay strong in faith at the same time. Like I've said before, you've got to become your own best cheerleader and get in position to experience restoration in your life.

As you study in the Word of God, you'll find that laughter is a sign of captivity being turned.

When the Lord turned again the captivity of Zion...

Then was our mouth filled with laughter, and our tongue with singing.

Psalm 126:1-2

When you see Christians laughing who haven't laughed in a long time, it's a sign that God is turning their captivity.

From the Book of Joel, we see God's people experience total disaster. They had never seen a devastation like this before. And God sends Joel right in the middle of it with a powerful message from God. The name Joel means "Yahweh is God." So when Joel shows up as God's representative, it literally means: Yahweh has come to town and will change everything. If Yahweh shows up at your house, devastation will be turned to restoration.

How many years have you been under Satan's attacks? How many years have you lived way below your privileges as a child of God? How many years have you lived in shame? Does it seem like the more money you make the more it's consumed and devoured before you can even enjoy it? Imagine Yahweh showing up at your house and saying, "I will restore to you everything." All the demons in hell will have to stand there and watch Yahweh turn devastation into restoration in your home.

Somebody said, "Well, why am I not receiving this refreshing and restoration?" Are you in position? Are you still complaining about the devastation? Do you have tunnel vision and all you can see is devastation? If so, then you're not in position to receive.

If all you can see is devastation and all you can talk about is devastation, then you're not in the presence of God. Let me show you something here in Joel 2:21. God is saying this. *Fear not, O land; be glad and rejoice: for the Lord will do great things."* Now notice He hadn't even said that *I will restore* yet— that came later. So apparently, if you're ever going to experience restoration and refreshing, then you must *be glad and rejoice* first.

Anybody can rejoice after restoration. Anybody can rejoice after a miracle. But that's not what God said. He didn't say, "I will restore, then you must be glad and rejoice." He said, "Be glad ye children of Zion and I will restore." Somebody said, "As soon as I get out of this mess, you talk about giving God a shout." That's backwards! That's like walking up to the fireplace and saying, "Give me some heat and I will throw in some wood." It doesn't work that way. You must throw in the wood first, and then it will produce heat. So, be glad and rejoice now, then you will see the restoration.

PERSPECTIVE & ATTITUDE

Refreshing and restoration are linked directly to your perspective and attitude about your circumstances. That's hard for some people. Many people are so negative about everything. You can say to some people, "Good Morning" and they'll say, "Hang around, it is not over yet." They will find something negative about everything.

The greatest expression of faith is thanksgiving and praise. Aren't we people of faith? Do we believe we receive when we pray? Then why do we wait to rejoice after the results come?

If someone said, "Brother Jerry, I'd like to buy you a new suit," being the gentleman that I am, the first thing I would do is say, "Thank you, that's very kind of you." I haven't even gotten the suit yet, but I'm already thanking that person. What would you think of me if I said, "Well, if you don't mind, I'll save the 'thank you' until I see it. As soon as I get the suit, then I'll say thank you." They have the right to say, "Forget it, you're not getting one. You need to learn some manners."

What is the most natural reaction if somebody says, "Hey, we'd like to take you to lunch?" "Thank you, that's very kind of you." You haven't even eaten yet, but you automatically give thanks. Why? Because you have faith in that person that they will do what they said.

If God tells you something, then you should say thank you in advance because He keeps His word. He's not a man that He should lie. He invented integrity. His word is His bond. He confirms His word with signs following. So I don't have to see it first. There are a lot of people in the body of Christ who need restoration. Marriages need restored. Families need restored. Finances need restored. Yet, they're waiting until they see restoration. "I'll get excited and I'll praise God and I'll give more when the restoration comes." God says, "No, you get excited and praise Me, and I will restore the years," hallelujah.

> *Fear not, O land; be glad and rejoice: for the Lord will do great things.*
>
> *Be glad then, ye children of Zion, and rejoice in the Lord your God: for he hath given you the former rain moderately, and he will cause to come down for you the rain, the former rain, and the latter rain in the first month.*
>
> *And the floors shall be full of wheat, and the vats shall overflow with wine and oil.*
>
> Joel 2:21,23-24

What's He saying? When Yahweh shows up, it doesn't make any difference how devastated your life is, He can change it in the twinkling of an eye.

The Bible tells us to enter into His presence with thanksgiving and praise. Start this act of getting in

His presence with thanksgiving and praise no matter what your circumstances might be. This puts pressure on the devil.

It just drives him up the wall when he has plotted and planned and schemed and set you up for the kill for months and months, and then when the attack is launched, you keep praising God anyway. He thinks he knows you better than that. He thinks you will be offended and will not pick up your Bible, nor listen to your tapes, nor read your books. That's what he thinks you will do. But when you praise God anyway, you make it hard on the devil!

Although the fig tree shall not blossom, neither shall fruit be in the vines; the labour of the olive shall fail, and the fields shall yield no meat; the flock shall be cut off from the fold, and there shall be no herd in the stalls:

Habakkuk 3:17

I'd say the boy's having a bad day. There's not one positive thing happening in this man's life. Notice, as an act of his own will he said,

Yet I will rejoice in the Lord, I will joy in the God of my salvation.

Habakkuk 3:18

What's he saying? You can destroy everything I have, take everything I have, do whatever you will, but there's one thing you will never steal from me and that's my joy, hallelujah. If Satan can't steal your joy, he cannot keep what he stole from you. It must be restored, hallelujah. And the prophet was saying, I don't care if I don't have one positive thing happening in my life, it will not get my joy. Somebody said, "Well, you just don't understand what I'm going through." No, that's not the issue here. You don't understand how powerful Yahweh is.

For example, every time God's people are devastated, God sends somebody with a joyful spirit. Haggai's name means, "festive spirit." You know what that tells me? When you've been devastated, overwhelmed with adversity, then you may not be able to go where there's someone with a festive spirit. That's the reason that you're going to have to develop your own festive spirit.

You've got to be your own Haggai, and then become a Haggai for somebody else. Become infectious. Become a carrier of joy.

No matter what you're going through, if you refuse to let it get your joy, then there is no way the devil can keep what he stole. He can't keep you down, praise God.

So start changing your outlook about your situation. Go ahead and give praise and thanksgiving to God right now before you even see any results of restoration. And then the Lord will do great things in your life.

CHAPTER 12

CHAPTER 12

The Best
is Yet To Come

You are so special to God that He thinks about you all the time. In fact, there is not another person on this planet who can take your place. It doesn't matter what your past is like, when God thinks about you, a smile comes on His face.

"Oh, but Brother Jerry, you don't realize what I've done in my life." It doesn't matter. God believes in what happened at Calvary even if no one else does. When God looks at you, He looks through the Blood of Jesus and sees someone that He loves very much, and He has great plans for your life!

Don't Limit God

God wants to do some BIG things in our lives, but they only happen in direct proportion to our ability to comprehend His great love for us. To *comprehend* means: to grasp, to catch hold of, to seize, to take in and to completely understand.

People who are unable to comprehend the love of God are limited as to how much they can receive from God. Can you truly say that you have a strong grip on how much God really loves you? Has your heart truly taken it in to the point that you completely understand?

Someone once said, "God loved us the way we were, but He loves us too much to leave us that way."

If you have truly comprehended this love, then you can no longer call yourself "worthless" or "nobody" or "just a worm in His sight". His love has made you the <u>righteousness of God.</u>

You are somebody special to Him! Not because of what you've done, but because of what Jesus did. Take it in, lay hold of it, seize this revelation. The larger it becomes on the inside of you, the more you'll expect from God.

Listen to Jesus, a man who knew that God loved Him.

I thank thee that thou hast heard me.

And I knew that thou hearest me always...

John 11:41-42

True comprehension of God's love causes you to know that He always hears you. You might say, "But that was Jesus." Yes, but listen to what He prayed for you and me.

In John 17:23 we read, *...hast loved them, as thou hast loved me.* God loves you and me just as much as He loves Jesus. Can you comprehend that? If not, then you'll always be limited as to how much of God's fullness you will receive.

The more you comprehend, the more of God's fullness you will experience. The more you comprehend, the more convinced you will become of your unlimited possibilities.

The Lord is gracious, and full of compassion; slow to anger, and of great mercy.

The Lord is good to all...

Psalm 145:8-9

"Full of compassion" means: to love tenderly, to be full of eager yearning. "The Lord is gracious" literally means: He is disposed to show favor.

Can you comprehend God's favor coming upon

you to the point that your life is blessed a thousand times more than it is right now? Before you answer, rebuke the temptation to say, "I can't imagine that." That's the problem!

This is why we've been so limited. We "can't imagine" because we haven't truly comprehended His love toward us. Comprehended love declares: "If God said it, that settles it and I can have it!"

I want you to know that you haven't seen your best days as a believer yet. They are not behind you - they are ahead of you. You have so much to look forward to in your life, but you've got to learn to stop limiting God. God's big! He's extravagant! He wants to bless you beyond what you ever thought before, but it will only happen when you stop thinking small!

Obviously, since you're reading this book, it could be that you need restoration in some area of your life. It could be in a family relationship; it could be in your marriage; it could be in the area of employment; or perhaps your finances. Well, let me tell you right now: Don't limit God!

Most of the time, we are the ones who limit God even though He is capable of doing so much more in our lives. For instance, look at the story in Psalm 78:6.

The people were stubborn and rebellious and they spoke against God even after He had done so many miraculous things in their lives.

Yea, they turned back and tempted God, and limited the Holy One of Israel.

Psalm 78:41

Even though God is unlimited, men can limit Him from doing mighty things in their lives.

In Mark 6:4-6, we see a similar example when Jesus entered His home town of Nazareth to preach to a group of people who only knew Him as the "carpenter's boy" and notice what happens.

But Jesus said unto them, A prophet is not without honour, but in his own country, and among his own kin, and in his own house.

And he could there do no mighty work, save that he laid his hands upon a few sick folk, and healed them.

And he marvelled because of their unbelief. And he went round about the villages, teaching.

The Message translation says, *Jesus wasn't able to do much of anything there...* Was Jesus any less anointed in Nazareth than He was in Capernaum? No. It was because the people didn't receive Him. They limited Him.

It's not because He is a respecter of persons. He's not. God's not going down the row saying, "I love thee, I love thee not...." He loves us all equally! God has no favorites! He will bless anyone who will allow Him to do so.

Psalm 115:12 says, *The Lord hath been mindful of us: he will bless us...* Look what's on the mind of God - US. God sits on His throne thinking of how He can bless us. And the Bible says that He never sleeps nor slumbers, so while we're sleeping, He's thinking up ways to bless us when we awake.

He said, "I'll bless you coming in, I'll bless you going out. I'll bless you in the city, and I'll bless you in the field..." God's got blessings chasing us down everywhere we go. If you say, "Well, my life's not like that. Nothing ever happens to me like that." It could be because of a lack of understanding of the Father's love.

FROM DEVASTATION TO RESTORATION

Psalm 115 continues to say,

...he will bless the house of Israel; he will bless the house of Aaron.

He will bless them that fear the Lord, both small and great.

The Lord shall increase you more and more, you and your children.

Psalm 115:12-14

God wants you to increase more and more. God is saying, "You haven't seen your best days yet!" His name is El Shaddai - not El Cheapo! The nature of God is to bless us. He can't help Himself! He does exceeding, abundantly above all that you could possibly ask or think. If you can think it, God says, "I can do exceeding, abundantly above that!" When you remove the limitations, you'll find that this extravagant God will do extravagant things in your life!

One of the greatest joys that Carolyn and I share is to see this work in our children. They've never been taught that miracles have passed away, and they are not for us today! All they know is that God is good! They have watched God do the miraculous in this family time and time again. They have never seen God disappoint this family. They have witnessed God's restoration in our lives. And now that they are adults and are having children of their own, it is a joy to see God doing the same things for them that He's done for us!

We've taught them that God's not against them, He is for them, and no weapon formed against them shall prosper! But we've also taught them that you don't "play church" with this. God wants total commitment. If you want to be blessed, then be totally committed to God. Put Him first! Don't pursue the blessings, pursue God and let the blessings pursue you! God said that the blessings will chase you down, come on you and overtake you!

So what is on the mind of God? You. Even when we disappoint Him, He still loves us. Even when we fall short, He still loves us. Why? Because He is long - suffering! He doesn't write us off when we make a mistake. He's the God of the second chance!

No matter what you are going through today, you have not seen your best days. Before you go to sleep tonight, the devil will try to convince you that there is no way out of your situation - you've had it. You're finished. It's over! Impossible! <u>But</u> God is saying: I'll never leave you nor forsake you.

God's already dreaming up a way to get you out of this devastation and turn every setback into a triumph! He'll turn every curse into a blessing and every stumbling block into a stepping stone for a greater victory! If you won't give up, you can walk right out of that situation praising God because He causes you to triumph always.

> *Being confident of this very thing, that he which hath begun a good work in you will perform it until the day of Jesus Christ.*

> Philippians 1:6

The Message translation says, *...bring it to a flourishing finish.* You have a "flourishing finish" awaiting you!

God wants to turn every test into a testimony! He wants to bless you no matter how impossible your situation may seem. In fact, He wants to bless you beyond your wildest dreams! He wants to restore every single thing Satan has stolen from you.

God can do anything, you know far more than you could ever imagine or guess or request in your wildest dreams!

Ephesians 3:20
(The Message)

This says to me that the best is yet to come! Get in position to receive. Get rid of all the limitations, and start expecting restoration as never before. As God's blessings increase in your life, then you can be a greater blessing to others. Your best days are just ahead of you! Make this your year for increase and restoration in every area of your life and begin to declare that the best is yet to come!

For Those Who Don't Know Jesus, Would You Like To Know Him?

If you were to die today, where would you spend eternity? If you have accepted Jesus Christ as your personal Lord and Savior, you can be assured that when you die, you will go directly into the presence of God in Heaven. If you have not accepted Jesus as your personal Lord and Savior, is there any reason why you can't make Jesus the Lord of your life right now? Please pray this prayer out loud, and as you do, pray with a sincere and trusting heart, and you will be born again.

Dear God in Heaven,

I come to You in the Name of Jesus to receive salvation and eternal life. I believe that Jesus is Your Son. I believe that He died on the cross for my sins, and that You raised Him from the dead. I receive Jesus now into my heart and make Him the Lord of my life. Jesus, come into my heart. I welcome You as my Lord and Savior. Father, I believe Your Word that says I am now saved. I confess with my mouth that I am saved and born again. I am now a child of God.

JSMI
Bible Institute
& School Of
World
Evangelism

Dear Friend,

Carolyn and I count it an honor to be involved in raising up students who will preach the uncompromised Word of God to the nations of the world. JSMI Bible Institute and School of World Evangelism is the fulfillment of a dream that was birthed in my spirit many years ago, and I am extremely excited about the potential we now have to train up students in an atmosphere charged with faith!

Our desire is to see each student develop a passion for God and a passion for souls. We endeavor to impart into each student the spirit of revival and help them become equipped and ready to participate in the last days move of God, bringing multitudes into His Kingdom.

If you are looking for a unique opportunity to increase your knowledge of the scriptures and find your place in God's plan, I trust you will prayerfully consider our school.

Sincerely,

Dr. Jerry Savelle

APPLICATION
REQUEST FORM

Please send me an application for JSMI Bible Institute and School Of World Evangelism

Name _____

Address _____

City/State _____

Zip/Telephone _____

To receive an application packet, please complete this form, tear it out and mail today.

**Jerry Savelle Ministries International
Bible Institute and School
of World Evangelism
P.O. Box 999
Crowley, TX 76036
817/297-2243 M-F 8:30-5:00 (CST)**

Other Books by Jerry Savelle

Walking In Divine Favor

Turning Your Dreams Into Reality

Turning Your Adversity Into Victory

Honoring Your Heritage Of Faith

Don't Let Go Of Your Dreams

Faith Building Daily Devotionals

The Force of Joy

If Satan Can't Steal Your Joy,
He Can't Keep Your Goods

A Right Mental Attitude

The Nature Of Faith

The Established Heart

Sharing Jesus Effectively

How To Overcome Financial Famine

You're Somebody Special To God

Leaving The Tears Behind

**For a complete list of tapes, books,
and videos by Jerry Savelle,
write or call:**

**Jerry Savelle Ministries International
P.O. Box 748
Crowley, Texas 76036
(817) 297-3155**